GoodNews EVANGEL

2022

Phillip A. Ross

Marietta, Ohio

ISBN: 978-1-7337267-5-7
Edition: 01.08.24

Published by

Pilgrim Platform
149 E. Spring St., Marietta
Ohio, 45750
www.pilgrim-platform.org

Biblical quotations are from the English Standard Version, Standard Bible Society, unless otherwise cited.

Printed in the United States of America

For
St. Paul's and the
evangelical catholic church
in the world over

Books by Phillip A. Ross

The Work At Zion—A Reckoning, Two-volume set, 772 pages, 1996.

Practically Christian—Applying James Today, 135 pages, 2006.

The Wisdom of Jesus Christ in the Book of Proverbs, 414 pages, 2006.

Marking God's Word—Understanding Jesus, 324 pages, 2006.

Acts of Faith—Kingdom Advancement, 326 pages, 2007.

Informal Christianity—Refining Christ's Church, 136 pages, 2007.

Engagement—Establishing Relationship in Christ, 104 pages, 1996, 2008.

It's About Time! — The Time Is Now, 40 pages. 2008.

The Big Ten—A Study of the Ten Commandments, 105 pages, 2001, 2008.

Arsy Varsy—Reclaiming The Gospel in First Corinthians, 406 pages, 2008.

Varsy Arsy—Proclaiming The Gospel in Second Corinthians, 356 pages, 2009.

Colossians—Christos Singularis, 278 pages, 2010.

Rock Mountain Creed—The Sermon on the Mount, 310 pages, 2011.

The True Mystery of the Mystical Presence, 355 pages, 2011.

Peter's Vision of Christ's Purpose in First Peter, 340 pages, 2011.

Peter's Vision of The End in Second Peter, 184 pages, 2012.

The Religious History of Nineteenth Century Marietta, Thomas Jefferson Summers, 124 pages, 1903, 2012 (editor).

Conflict of Ages—The Great Debate of the Moral Relations of God and Man, Edward Beecher, 489 pages, 1853, 2012 (editor).

Concord Of Ages—The Individual And Organic Harmony Of God And Man, Edward Beecher, D. D., 524 pages, 1860, 2013 (editor).

Ephesians—Recovering the Vision of a Sustainable Church in Christ, 417 pages, 2013.

Galatians: Backstory/Christory, 315 pages, 2015.

Poet Tree—Root, Branch & Sap, 72 pages, 2013.

Inside Out Woman—Collected Poetry, Doris M. Ross, 195 pages, 2014 (editor).

God's Great Plan for the World—The Biblical Story of Creation and Redemption, 305 pages, 2019.

John's Miracles—Seeing Beyond Our Expectations, 210 pages, 2019.

Essays on Church—Ordinary Christianity for the World, 385 pages, 2020.

Thessalonians—Thorn, Thistle, and Thrown, 160 pages, 2021.

Institutes of The Christian Religion, Emanuel V. Gerhart, 9 volumes, 2023 (editor).

Goodnews—Evangel 2022, 187 pages, 2023

TABLE OF CONTENTS

INTRODUCTION

My wife and I began attending St. Paul's about 10-12 years ago, when Rev. Thomas Hendershot was the pastor. We came to Marietta in 1996 to serve Putnam Congregational Church in Devola, and did so for about four years. We then decided to remain in Marietta, bought a house, and I opened my own business.

I was an early adopter to the computer revolution and bought an Apple II in 1984 and read my weight in computer magazines. My business utilized computers as I developed a local desktop publishing business and over the years added promotional products, graphic and website design to my services.

During those years I also led a small church start with a few people. Over time it became a home church, which I gave up when I joined Covenant Presbyterian Church in America, a new church start in Vienna, West Virginia, about twenty minutes from home. I was not the pastor of that church, but became an elder, and was the only remaining elder when that church closed in 2004 or so. A few of us continued a weekly Bible study for a few years. We decided that we needed to find a church, and after looking around, each family went its own way. Our families were geographically distant from one another. Stephanie and I began to attend, and shortly thereafter, joined St. Paul's.

During all of that time I continued to write and publish my books. St. Paul's Evangelical Church came from the same historic tradition that I did, the United Church of Christ (UCC), in which I was ordained and served for about fifteen years. The UCC continued to drift liberal, and I continued to grow more conservative, so we parted ways in 1995. Putnam was my first church in my new denomination, the Conservative Congregational Christian Conference (CCCC), a small Congregational splinter that was founded in 1947. My history was Congregational from my childhood, and history is important. By joining the CCCC I could continue my Congregational trajectory. I continue my CCCC membership today.

I served as Interim Pastor at St. Paul's when Pastor Tom left, and nurtured Rev. Josef Vasarhelyi, a newly graduated seminarian as he led St. Paul's. Pastor Joe was well-loved at St. Paul's, though he had a difficult time. St. Paul's has a long history of short pastorates, and over its 185 year history has belonged to seven different denominational groups.

Originally, St. Paul's was associated with a group headquartered in Germany. In 1870 it affiliated with an American German denomination, the German Evangelical Synod of North America. In 1934 that denomination united with another German American church and St. Paul's became affiliated with the Evangelical and Reformed Church. In 1957 that church body united with the General Council of the Congregational Christian Churches to form the United Church of Christ.

The UCC continued to drift in a liberal and unbiblical direction, while St. Paul's held fast to its tradition theology and beliefs. And over time that relationship became untenable. Unhappy with the ministers provided by the UCC, St. Paul's began finding local pastors for pulpit supply.

Rev. Steve Dennis had been filling in at St. Luke's Lutheran, across the alley from St. Paul's. And he became available to St. Paul's. They liked him, though he was a Lutheran and a member of Lutheran Churches In Mission (LCIM), a conservative splinter group of the mainline Lutherans. Pastor Dennis became the longest serving pastor at St. Paul's. But St. Paul's did not want to become Lutheran.

Tom Hendershot had grown up around Marietta, and had served a career in the U.S. Army as a Chaplain. He had returned to Marietta after his service to care for his elderly mother. He, then, became the Pastor of St. Paul's, and worked to renew, rebuild, and revive the church by focusing on the church's original history, traditions, and theology, which was German Evangelical. The German Evangelical in Germany was neither Catholic nor Lutheran, but was composed of the various Calvinist and successor churches in Germany. Tom's research led him to the Evangelical Association of Reformed and Congregational Churches (EA), another splinter group composed of mostly former UCC churches of the Evangelical And Reformed side of the UCC merger. St. Paul's is currently affiliated with the EA, as it is affectionately known.

When Pastor Joe Vasarhelyi left, I again became the Interim. At this point St. Paul's had gone through some difficulties and several families left, leaving a very small congregation. St. Paul's could not afford another full-time pastor, and it would be years before we could. So I stepped in to help renew, rebuild, and revive the church. St. Paul's had been through several life cycles over its long history, and will recover.

I have been learning about St. Paul's history and the history and theology of the German Evangelical church. It is quite interesting, and able to provide the restoration that St. Paul's and the American churches generally need. My writing and preaching is in the vein of that restoration. Lord, have mercy.

Over the years I have converted many of my preaching sermon series on various books of the Bible into books. But following some church difficulties at St. Paul's I didn't have a clear idea about what to preach. So I decided to follow the Lectionary, which has provided timely, appropriate, and interesting messages. I pray that they will speak to you as they have spoken to me.

Phillip A. Ross
Marietta, Ohio
2023

Put On Christ

I was ready to be sought by those who did not ask for me; I was ready to be found by those who did not seek me. I said, "Here I am, here I am," to a nation that was not called by my name. 2 I spread out my hands all the day to a rebellious people, who walk in a way that is not good, following their own devices; 3 a people who provoke me to my face continually, sacrificing in gardens and making offerings on bricks; 4 who sit in tombs, and spend the night in secret places; who eat pig's flesh, and broth of tainted meat is in their vessels; 5 who say, "Keep to yourself, do not come near me, for I am too holy for you." These are a smoke in my nostrils, a fire that burns all the day. 6 Behold, it is written before me: "I will not keep silent, but I will repay; I will indeed repay into their lap 7 both your iniquities and your fathers' iniquities together, says the Lord; because they made offerings on the mountains and insulted me on the hills, I will measure into their lap payment for their former deeds." 8 Thus says the Lord: "As the new wine is found in the cluster, and they say, 'Do not destroy it, for there is a blessing in it,' so I will do for my servants' sake, and not destroy them all. 9 I will bring forth offspring from Jacob, and from Judah possessors of my mountains; my chosen shall possess it, and my servants shall dwell there. —Isaiah 65:1-9

23 Now before faith came, we were held captive under the law, imprisoned until the coming faith would be revealed. 24 So then, the law was our guardian until Christ came, in order that we might be justified by faith. 25 But now that faith has come, we are no longer under a guardian, 26 for in Christ Jesus you are all sons of God, through faith. 27 For as many of you as were baptized into Christ have put on Christ. 28 There is neither Jew nor Greek, there is nei-

> *ther slave nor free, there is no male and female, for you are all one in Christ Jesus. 29 And if you are Christ's, then you are Abraham's offspring, heirs according to promise.* —*Galatians 3:23-29*

As I was contemplating this message and considering the text from Isaiah, it seemed to me that it is important for us to hear today what the Lord says about unfaithfulness through Isaiah. It's not pleasant because it is convicting, which is why it is important to hear what the Lord says. I am making a point to bring this message because it is my understanding, my observation, that people in general don't know Scripture very well. That is the fault of churches and pastors, and it is the responsibility of churches and pastors to correct. People need to become more familiar with the Bible; we need to hear it often. This is one of the things I do in my preaching and writing.

In this second reading from Galatians Paul says that Christ has not abrogated the law, which means is that the law still stands. It was a guardian for God's people, to protect us. And the law still stands as a testimony to the righteousness of the Lord and of His law. Christ did not come to destroy the law, but came to fulfill the law. So while the law still stands, it stands in a different kind of relationship for people in Christ than it does for people not in Christ. And to see what that means we need to go back to Galatians 3:3-6, to the context. There Paul wrote:

> *"O foolish Galatians! Who has bewitched you? It was before your eyes that Jesus Christ was publicly portrayed as crucified. 2 Let me ask you only this: Did you receive the Spirit by works of the law or by hearing with faith? 3 Are you so foolish? Having begun by the Spirit, are you now being perfected by the flesh? 4 Did you suffer so many things in vain—if indeed it was in vain? 5 Does he who supplies the Spirit to you and works miracles among you do so by works of the law, or by hearing with faith—6 just as Abraham 'believed God, and it was counted to him as righteousness'"?*

Paul was responding to some unfaithfulness in the Galatian church. They were unfaithful because they were confused. Christ had died, and they were deeply grieved. We should not blame them for their confusion. In their situation we would have done no better. Paul was trying to straighten that out. Many of them, some of whom were Jewish, wanted to return to their practice of strict obedience to the law as the means of salvation. Of course they lifted that up as a goal, but never did—nor could—actually achieve salvation through obedience to the law. It was an unachievable goal, so Paul was correcting that mistaken idea.

He said, *no, no! That is not what it is about.* Christ has made many very significant changes in this world since Paul wrote to the Galatians. So while our world is very different from Paul's, we are not so different. In our day people are also confused, and for a similar reason: The Galatians didn't know the New Testament. How could they? I was in the process of being written, and Paul's letter to the Galatians was very early in his writing.

Today when we watch the news or listen to people in our world, we begin thinking: *what in the world has happened to our world?* It seems our contemporary world been completely transformed, seemingly overnight. Of course, in reality this transformation of our world of contemporary America, this transformation into godlessness, has actually been happening for quite a long time. But of late more and more people are coming to see it. They're coming to realize it. They're coming to understand that what God said in the past is true. The problem is that we Americans haven't really believed Him. But suddenly it seems to be true because it's coming to fruition.

But the thing I want to share with you this morning about contemporary faithlessness and the encroaching darkness of the world is that God is still on the throne. And God is good! God has always been good. And God is still on the throne.

So the takeaway here is that the worse the world gets, the more the goodness of the gospel is going to stand out in contrast to the malady of the darkness. Whereas in the past we didn't realize how bad the world was and is, so we didn't actually realize how good the gospel is either. People haven't paid much attention to the gospel over the last fifty or a hundred years. We have excised the Bible out of our colleges, universities, and public education. But as the world gets darker, and because Christ is still on the throne, because God is sovereign, we must realize that *God* is bringing all of this darkness about. Not for our destruction, but for our benefit. But in order to benefit we must understand what God is doing.

In addition, I believe that a large group of people, who knows how many, will soon come to see the truth of the gospel against the background of the darkness of godlessness that is in our world today. The increasing darkness is going to make the gospel shine all the more clear. It's already beginning to happen for people who have eyes to see and ears to hear.

God is allowing this darkness to come, to manifest in our world. It's a function of His revelation. The darkness is part of His revelation. How so? Were seeing what is actually going on in the world better—more clearly—than we were seeing it before. And we don't like it! It's dark. It's ugly. It's truly depressing. But the gospel hasn't changed. The brokenness of our world is becoming more clear. But God is still good.

This means that there is a tremendous opportunity lying at our doorstep for faithful Christians and faithful churches to simply *be faithful*. You see, a faithful church in the midst of the darkness of the world will simply reveal the truth of God's goodness. Not perfectly, in fits and starts, here and there. But our simple faithfulness will begin to reveal the truth of God against the darkness of faithlessness. God's truth is coming as a blessing. But God's truth is also coming to convict the world, to convict you and me, to show us our errors, our own faithlessness.

Last week our scripture lesson came out of John 16. And it included these verses:

> *"And when he comes, he will convict the world concerning sin and righteousness and judgment: concerning sin, because they do not believe in me. 10 concerning righteousness, because I go to the Father, and you will see me no longer; concerning judgment, because the ruler of this world is judged. I still have many things to say to you, but you cannot bear them now. When the Spirit of truth comes, he will guide*

> *you into all the truth, for he will not speak on his own authority, but whatever he hears he will speak, and he will declare to you the things that are to come." (John 16:8-13).*

Those are the words of Jesus, but the fulfillment of those words was the ministry of Paul. Paul, who wrote eighty percent of the New Testament, presented the spirit of truth. And here we see that Paul is guiding God's people into all truth. So what we can discern from this? We can make use of this insight by going back to Paul's words and read them, understand them, study them, knowing that they apply to us right now.

In this, there is a great opportunity on our doorstep. And we don't actually have to do much to manifest it, to make use of it. We don't have to go anywhere. We don't have to spend any extra money. All we have to do is be faithful, hang in there, and trust the Lord. We simply need to continue doing what we've been doing for a long time. But we need to do it better; we need to know the Bible better. But mostly we simply need to *be faithful* right here, right now, where we are.

From all of this we can experientially see how God's law, knowing God's Word, served as a guardian for ancient Israel. God's Word was given in order to guard Israel from its own destruction. It was to guard Israel from the consequences of unfaithfulness. If you read and study the Bible, you will see that ancient Israel, in the long run, turned out to *not* be faithful in lots of ways, over many generations. And it finally got to the point that God sent Jesus Christ to do for them what they could not do for themselves, what we cannot do for ourselves.

Part of ancient Israel's unfaithfulness was the keeping of God's Word for themselves. They mistakenly thought that God would only save faithful Jews. The ended up trying to keep the blessings of God's Word to themselves, for themselves. But that was never what God intended. The ancient Jews were to be a blessing for the world. They were to model faithfulness, and share that model with the world. But they failed to do this.

In consequence God took the Jewish nation off the playing field through the destruction of Jerusalem and the destruction of the Temple in A.D. 70. Israel then had no homeland for two thousand years. God simply took them off the playing field. They then wandered aimlessly in the world trying to hold on to what they thought was true, but never quite came to realize who Jesus Christ actually is.

That part of the story is still happening, still unfolding. We're still in it. So the consequence of their unfaithfulness was the loss of the temple in Jerusalem and their homeland in A.D. 70. There is a harsh lesson in all of this because Israel was God's chosen people, His special people. He nurtured them, He gave them everything. He gave them grace, He gave them the law, He gave them the traditions. He took them out of Egypt, and protected them in the desert. But it didn't work, it wasn't enough. Why not? Did God not know what he was doing?

No, God knew very well what he was doing. So why did God allow the ancient Israelites to be faithless? He was teaching them, teaching the world, teaching *us*, the importance of Jesus Christ the Messiah by withholding that Messiah from them. He showed us what happens when Christ is not available. He then gave His Messiah, Jesus Christ, to the world. He did it for *us*, he did it for future generations, so that we could look at them and learn from them. He was trying to teach His people, teach us, teach all Christians—everybody in the world—about justification by faith, and the problem with justification by works.

The lesson is that in Christ we are given faith because we are unable to earn it or achieve it by our own efforts. We cannot make it happen. But we can receive a gift that's been freely given to us. So following what Paul said here in the third chapter of Galatians, how are people then included in Christ? Paul says,

> *"For as many of you as were baptized into Christ Jesus you have put on Christ" (Galatians 3:27).*

Through baptism people are included into Christ. But the doctrine and practice of baptism has given the church fits for many,

many centuries. What is it? How do you do it? What's the right way? Children? Only adults? Sprinkling, pouring, immersion? Etc. But Paul's discussion of baptism included more than the ceremony of baptism. Paul also talked about the reality of baptism as a personal, spiritual reality.

And here, Paul was not talking about the ceremony of baptism and how we might exercise that ceremony. Paul was talking about what we might call the *fruit* of baptism, which is new life. It's the reality of being born again into a new life, which the ceremony of baptism symbolizes as the beginning of that new life. So Paul was more interested in the reality of new life than in the ceremony of baptism, and we can learn from that as well.

Of course, we also understand that faithful believers are normally ceremonially baptized, and that ceremony is important. But the other thing that we realize from the multitude of churches and different ways of doing baptism today is that there are a lot of different ways to do the ceremony. And the symbolism is different for the different ways of doing it, but in a sense they all present important and valuable, but different sorts of symbolism.[1]

However, the reality is the new life in Christ that has begun in the individual, not the ceremony. Of course, the ceremony is important. Baptism is like marriage. My mom would say something like this: *A wedding does not a marriage make*. She liked to talk like that. The wedding is just the ceremony. But the marriage is what happens over the life of the individuals, and that's the main thing.

Paul says that in our baptism we *put on Christ*. Well, what does he mean: *put on Christ*? It's like you put on a coat. And, in a sense, that is what he means. You put it on. You wear it. And by this he means that we are to take on the character qualities of Jesus Christ. When I put on a coat and then present myself to the world or meet people in public, the first thing that you see is what I'm wearing, my clothes.

So if we put on Christ in the same way as wearing a coat, when we meet with each other or anybody in public or in private, the first

1 See "Baptism Parallels" in the Appendix of *Ephesians—Recovering The Vision Of As Sustainable Church In Christ*, Phillip A. Ross, Pilgrim Platform, Marietta, Ohio, 2012.

thing that they should see is … what? The first thing that people should see is the character qualities of Jesus Christ *in us*. By wearing them we show them to others. Others should see the character qualities of Christ in us. That's how we put them on. We put them on by practicing them. We are to manifest the fruits of the spirit in our own lives, in our own churches.

Love joy, peace, patience, forbearance, kindness, goodness, faithfulness, gentleness, and self-control (Galatians 5:28-9). That's one list. It's not inclusive. There are others, but that's a heck of a good place to start. But there is more. Paul also says,

> *"There is neither Jew nor Greek, there is neither slave nor free, there is no male and female, for you are all one in Christ Jesus" (Galatians 3:28).*

You are all one in Christ Jesus. We worry about the unity of the church an awful lot in today's world. Mostly because we've spent fifty or a hundred years now trying to manifest that unity among the various churches ,and it hasn't gone very well. We haven't done it. But again, what did Paul say? You *are* all one in Christ. What did Paul not say? You *will be* one in Christ. He said you *are* one in Christ. It's already true. We don't actually need to do anything to become one in Christ, to be one with other Christians, to be in unity with other Christians.

Well, that's not quite true because we do have to put on Christ. If we put on Christ, then that puts us in union with other Christians because we are already in unity with Christ. If we try to be in unity with one another, then I either have to conform to your ways, or you have to conform to my ways. And that doesn't work out very well. But if we can agree that we both have to conform to Christ's ways, then the closer we get to Christ, the closer we get to one another. That's the unity that Jesus Christ is talking about.

Thus, the effort, our effort, to bring about denominational unity in the churches in this world is futile. Our efforts are futile because unity belongs to the category of eternity. We only find unity when we are connected with Christ who is eternal. And this means that there is an eternal part of us that is connected with an eternal part of

Christ. My eternal part connects with Christ's eternal part through the power and presence of the Holy Spirit. To be in unity with Christ is to be in unity with His Body, the church.

So as individuals we can grow in union with Jesus Christ. We can grow closer to Christ, which will bring us closer to one another. Yes, we are already in union, but we can grow more deeply in that union. And the more we grow closer to Christ, the more we will grow closer to one another, to others who are growing in Christ.

However, it seems that our earthly churches cannot be in unity with other churches, nor with Christ because our earthly churches are temporal institutions. Our earthly churches are not going to make it to heaven. Our earthly churches are just worldly organizations, 501c3 corporations if you will. Our earthly churches are temporal, not eternal. And to try to make a temporal thing an eternal thing is a fool's errand. And we've been chasing after that fool's errand for too long.

Yet our unity in Christ is real. So, in order to have unity with other individual Christians all we really need to do is to be in unity with Christ personally, here and now. Paul says, because Christ says, we are one in Jesus Christ. But how does this work in the world? Is everybody just going to believe what I have said here? Fat chance! That's not going to happen. But the good news is that you don't have to believe *me*. You just have to believe *Jesus*.

But what about those people that don't believe Jesus, that don't believe the Bible, that don't practice Christianity? What about them? Well that's an interesting issue because at this point it seems like there are a lot of them. So what do we do with them? What do we do with unbelievers? My best advice again comes out of Scripture. And here's what Scripture says, (coming back to Isaiah):

> *"Come, everyone who thirsts, come to the waters; and he who has no money, come, buy and eat! Come, buy wine and milk without money and without price. 2 Why do you spend your money for that which is not bread, and your labor for that which does not satisfy? Listen diligently to me, and eat what is good, and delight yourselves in rich food. 3 Incline your ear, and come to me; hear, that your soul may live; and*

I will make with you an everlasting covenant, my steadfast, sure love for David" (Isaiah 55:1-3).

This is written, not simply to the church, not simply to practicing Christians. Of course it is intended for the church, but it also reaches beyond the church. It is written to the world. *Come everybody who thirsts!* Who doesn't thirst? Everybody thirsts. Come, taste it, try it!

"O taste and see that the Lord is good. Blessed is the man who takes refuge in him" (Psalm 34:8).

As they used to say in a TV commercial: *try it, you'll like it.* That's my best advice for people. If you don't believe the Bible, if you don't believe Jesus, if you're really interested, if you want to know the truth: *try it.* Try obeying a couple of things that Jesus says. Try putting on His character qualities, the fruits of the spirit. Just try it in your family, try it with your friends and see how that works. See if imitating the character qualities of Jesus is helpful. Just try it. Don't trust me. Try it yourself.

And in this simple message, a faithful church has got a great message for the world. It's really fairly simple. We don't have to go anywhere. We don't have to do much of anything. We don't have to spend any money. We just need to be faithful. Can we do that? Amen.

Heavenly Father, we are grateful for the blessings that you have provided for us, for your love and grace and mercy and wisdom. We thank you that you have been with us in our own lives over the years, for many of us you have been with us over the decades, for some of us over practically a lifetime. And for this church, over several lifetimes. So we are thankful, Father, for your presence. Help us to celebrate your presence. When we celebrate Jesus Christ as *our* Lord and Savior. Help us to celebrate your presence among us here in this church. But not just in this church, not just inside the church, be with us even when we leave here. Help us to take our celebration of Jesus Christ, our remembering of Jesus Christ with us as we go. It is the gift that you have given us. You have given us the

Holy Spirit that through His activity in our life, we can remember who you are and who you created us to be, and how we can live more fully.

So we pray for this church and the transitions and the new chapter that you have for this church. We don't know the future, but we trust the one who does. Help us to trust you, Father. Help us to lean into your future and your faithfulness for us here in this time and in this place.

We pray for your mercy, but we also pray that you would help us to be faithful, Father. We are aware that Marietta has a long history and a long involvement with the founding of this nation. Father, help us to just be faithful, to show the world that that's really all you're looking for. And if a lot of people are just a little bit faithful, that will manifest into a lot of faith. So help us to do that here.

We pray for this nation and for our political leaders, and we are aware that the war is heating up again, and we pray against the war. We pray for peace, the peace that you have promised us. So we pray for our leaders that they would manifest your truth and your fruits in their lives, and be examples for the rest of us. And also help us to be examples to them, come what may.

We pray for mercy, Father, mercy as you bring the fullness of Jesus Christ into the darkness of this world. We know that it's for our good. We know that it's for a blessing that will give you glory and give us peace and health and hope and love and all that you have promised. So help us to be serious about that in our prayers. We pray all of this in Jesus' name, Amen.

June 19, 2022

Freedom

*51 When the days drew near for him to be taken up, he set his face to
go to Jerusalem. 52 And he sent messengers ahead of him, who went
and entered a village of the Samaritans, to make preparations for him.
53 But the people did not receive him, because his face was set toward Jerusalem. 54 And when his disciples James and John saw it,
they said, "Lord, do you want us to tell fire to come down from
heaven and consume them?"55 But he turned and rebuked them. 56
And they went on to another village. 57 As they were going along
the road, someone said to him, "I will follow you wherever you go."
58 And Jesus said to him, "Foxes have holes, and birds of the air
have nests, but the Son of Man has nowhere to lay his head." 59 To
another he said, "Follow me." But he said, "Lord, let me first go and
bury my father." 60 And Jesus said to him, "Leave the dead to bury
their own dead. But as for you, go and proclaim the kingdom of
God." 61 Yet another said, "I will follow you, Lord, but let me first
say farewell to those at my home." 62 Jesus said to him, "No one
who puts his hand to the plow and looks back is fit for the kingdom
of God.* *—Luke 9:51-62*

*13 For you were called to freedom, brothers. Only do not use your
freedom as an opportunity for the flesh, but through love serve one
another. 14 For the whole law is fulfilled in one word: "You shall
love your neighbor as yourself." 15 But if you bite and devour one
another, watch out that you are not consumed by one another. 16 But
I say, walk by the Spirit, and you will not gratify the desires of the
flesh. 17 For the desires of the flesh are against the Spirit, and the de-*

> *sires of the Spirit are against the flesh, for these are opposed to each*
> *other, to keep you from doing the things you want to do. 18 But if*
> *you are led by the Spirit, you are not under the law. 19 Now the*
> *works of the flesh are evident: sexual immorality, impurity, sensuality,*
> *20 idolatry, sorcery, enmity, strife, jealousy, fits of anger, rivalries, dis-*
> *sensions, divisions, 21 envy, drunkenness, orgies, and things like these.*
> *I warn you, as I warned you before, that those who do such things will*
> *not inherit the kingdom of God. 22 But the fruit of the Spirit is love,*
> *joy, peace, patience, kindness, goodness, faithfulness, 23 gentleness,*
> *self-control; against such things there is no law. 24 And those who be-*
> *long to Christ Jesus have crucified the flesh with its passions and de-*
> *sires. 25 If we live by the Spirit, let us also keep in step with the*
> *Spirit.* —*Galatians 5:13-25*

Luke says, "But the people did not receive him because his face was set toward Jerusalem." This reminds me of the story of the woman in the well (John 4). If you remember that story, Jesus was out, and at midday He went to the well and talked to this woman who was a Samaritan, who had all the husbands. I'm sure you remember the story.

But at one point in their conversation, the issue of worship came up, and she said that because she was a Samaritan, that she worshiped at Mount Gerizim, not at the temple in Jerusalem. Again, the history is important. The Samaritan history went back several centuries to the time when Israel had been routed. The Assyrians destroyed Jerusalem and took all of the wealthy and successful Jews back to Assyria because they wanted to use them for their own purposes. They became Assyrian slaves. And they left the rest of the people in Israel.

The remaining Jews over the centuries built their own worship center in Samaria because the Temple in Jerusalem had been destroyed. The used what they could remember of the old temple And these people then became known as Samaritans, who had their own worship center at Mount Gerizim, which was in competition with the old temple establishment at Jerusalem.

So the Samaritans were actually Jews who were worshiping at another temple. Each side, Samaria and Jerusalem, thought that the other side was faithless. That was the problem with the Samaritans. And of course, archeology has recently uncovered the remains of a temple complex on Mount Gerizim, so we know that the story is true. The Samaritans also had their own high priest, and they carried out what they thought were all of the Temple duties found in the Old Testament books of Moses.

When Jesus said that He set His face to Jerusalem, the Samaritans said, *well, that's not good because you're going to Jerusalem, but the true church (from the Samaritan perspective) is at Mount Gerizim*. That was the source of the conflict with the woman at the well. That's why the Samaritans didn't accept Him at first. Jesus was making a stand at Jerusalem. Jesus had set His face to go to Jerusalem.

Why was He going to Jerusalem? To die? Well, that wasn't very popular with anyone. The disciples didn't like it either. The Messiah shouldn't go off and die in such a way. So the disciples didn't respond as they heard this. They said, *well, do you think we ought to just bring fire down upon these faithless Samaritans?* That's very typical. The disciples wanted to rebuke them, to cause them pain, to destroy them. And Jesus said, *no, no, we don't do that.* We're not going to bring in firepower. Then Jesus talked about foxes and birds.

And the point that Jesus was making here was that the Son of Man had no place to sleep, no home. He was a wandering itinerant teacher. He had no home. He slept at other people's homes, so we might call him homeless. And that wasn't what they expected either.

Christians today often have the same thoughts as this teacher of the law who thought that Jesus ought to be better equipped, and have all the stuff He needs. We often expect that we can follow Jesus and still have all of our money and all of our comforts, and all of the stuff that money buys.

Jesus is saying that there's nothing wrong with that, but it can get in the way. And so He was preparing His disciples for difficulty that was coming because He knew that shortly after His death, they would be persecuted as well.

So another person comes along and says, well, *I'll follow you, but my dad just died and I've got to go to the funeral and all that stuff*. And Jesus said, *let the dead bury the dead.* It doesn't sound very friendly, actually. It doesn't sound all that spiritual either, because we need to honor the dead. We need to have funerals.

The point that Jesus was trying to make is that the people of the world are dead to Christ. They don't see Christ's beauty. They don't hear His voice, and they don't desire to follow Him. Only His sheep will do the things that He tells them to do. Only His sheep can hear Him. So if *you* can hear Jesus, you know that you are a sheep of His.

But it is also really important to honor our parents. That's the fifth commandment; we are to honor mother and father. But Jesus was saying, at this particular point in His ministry, that the presentation of the gospel was more important than honoring their parents.

Then another person came to Him and Jesus responded to him,

> *"No one who puts his hand to the plow and looks back is fit for the kingdom of God" (Luke 9:62).*

We don't do much hand plowing anymore, but it used to be in those days that you wrapped a leather strap around yourself to hold the plow, and had a horse or ox pulling the plow. Your job was to plow a straight line, which meant that you could not look away from what you were doing. If you didn't keep your eye on where you were going, your plow line wouldn't be straight.

The point is that you had to keep your eye on where you were going at all times. That's the point Jesus was making. We need to keep our eyes on Jesus. We need to not look back at what has already happened. All that stuff is in the past. An old Chinese proverb says, *water downstream cannot be used to turn the mill*. Let it go. The past is gone. It can't help you.

Another lesson in this section is that a person who didn't finish the job that God had given him will not be fit for the kingdom. How can God entrust His kingdom to us if we are looking elsewhere, if we're not keeping our eyes on Him? If we're looking back to what happened and feeling bad about ourselves, we will lose it all. We need to let all that stuff go. In Christ we are called to freedom.

And that brings us to the Galatians scripture.

> *"For you were called to freedom, brothers. Only do not use your freedom as an opportunity for the flesh, but through love serve one another" (Galatians 5:13-14).*

Consider our freedom. Yet, while we are free, we are not called to do what *we* want to do with our freedom. We are called to do what *God* wants us to do with our freedom. Paul goes on to say that the whole law is fulfilled when we love our neighbor as ourselves. He says that the whole law is summed up in that one command.

But elsewhere, Jesus says that the law is summed up in *two* commands. Here Paul says *one* command; elsewhere, Scripture says *two*, and that's caused some confusion.

> *"You shall love the Lord your God with all your heart and with all your soul and with all your mind. This is the great and first commandment. And a second is like it: You shall love your neighbor as yourself. On these two commandments depend all the Law and the Prophets" (Matthew 22:37-40.*

Because the two commands come from Jesus, and the one command comes from Paul, we should go with the two commands. Because in order to genuinely love our neighbor, we have to genuinely love God first. God is first always.

Paul goes on to say that the spirit and the flesh are opposed to one another. And really what he's saying there is that the people of the spirit and people of the flesh are opposed to one another. They have different sets of values. If you are a Christian, you have one set of values. If you are not a Christian, you have a completely different set of values. And the two sets of values are at odds with one another. We are beginning to see that this is true more and more in our world today.

However, Paul was not saying that God is opposed to everything of the flesh. God is not opposed to eating. God is not opposed to having money. It's what you do with your money that creates conflicts with God. It's not how much money you have, it's what you do with what you have. Similarly, God is not opposed to sex. It's what you do with these things, how you use them, that creates conflicts with God.

Nonetheless, Scripture says that the spirit and the flesh are opposed to one another. And in the early centuries of Christianity, there was confusion about this and people went to off and became hermits and monks, and tried to completely avoid everybody. During these years ascetic Christianity was promoted. But Jesus was not an ascetic. He loved life!

Clearly, leading an ascetic life is not right because God calls us to love one another, not to avoid one another. And you can't love one another if you go off and live like a hermit. Love requires us to be engaged with people. Consequently, we have come to learn that there is nothing wrong with our fleshly appetites as long as we keep them in control and in service to God—in line with Christ in His teachings.

Paul goes on to say,

> *"For the desires of the flesh are against the Spirit, and the desires of the Spirit are against the flesh, for these are opposed to each other, to keep you from doing the things you want to do" (Galatians 5:17).*

What does that mean? It goes back to the whole idea of original sin. If you remember in the garden God said there are two trees, the tree of life and the tree of the knowledge of good and evil. We are to eat of the tree of life, and not to eat of the tree of the knowledge of good and evil.

But Satan came along and said to Eve, *God doesn't know what He's talking about. That tree is pretty good.* So Eve looked at it and said, *it looks good, tastes good, and I believe it will make me wise.* Notice that she imposed her own desires and preferences on what she should do. And she abandoned what God had said. God said, *don't eat it.* She said, *it looks pretty good to me.*

The lesson in this is that there is an important sense that the spirit and the flesh are opposed to one another. And the purpose of that opposition is to keep us from doing the things we want to do, from imposing our will on God's instructions. God wants us to put His will, His values first. We are in service of him. He is not in service of us. And this is an important issue, and we are forever getting it confused.

So then Paul went on to say how the works of the flesh are evident. And he has a list that is shocking. His list shows us where concerns of the flesh supersede concerns of the spirit. Here is his list: sexual immorality, yeah, we're all good with that. Impurity, sensuality, idolatry, sorcery, enmity, strife, jealousy, fits of anger, rivalries, dissensions, visions, envy, drunkenness, orgies, and things like these (Galatians 5: 19-20).

Think carefully about this list. He says none of that, none of the people who engage in those kinds of things will receive the kingdom. This is a tough list. We tend to single out a couple of them, and ignore the rest. We'll focus on sexual immorality—those folks are out for sure! Idolatry—those folks are out. Sorcery—no question, they are out.

But what about jealousy, anger, rivalry, dissension, envy, etc.? These things are hitting pretty close to home—fits of anger, rivalries, dissensions? If you take this list of characteristics seriously you won't find anybody who isn't on it. We're all on Paul's list to not receive the kingdom! And that's the point. We were all immersed and engaged in serious sin apart from Christ.

But, said Paul, *when we are in Christ then we are freed from our old habits, our old ways of living.* We are freed from doing those things out of habit, and in Christ we can then begin to change our habits and start following God. Knowing that doing those things will keep us from the kingdom of God, but following Christ will provide the kingdom of God.

Paul set up this contrast between faithfulness and unfaithfulness, between not being in Christ and being in Christ. First he said, *don't do these things.* And he listed these negative things. Then he said, *I want you to do these things.* And he named the fruits of the Spirit. Through the Spirit is joy.

> *"Love, joy, peace, patience, kindness, goodness, faithfulness, gentleness, self-control. Against such things there is no law (Galatians 5:22-23).*

Rather than doing those things on the first list he wants us to engage the things on this second list. And that is what we do in the church. As we gather to worship we lift these things up, and we teach about them, and we talk about them. And we gather together in fellowship we practice them so that when we get out into the world we will be able to do them better. That is what the Lord is calling us to do and to be in His church in this time and in this place.

Lord, help us to be who you have called us to be. Give us wisdom and instruction and help us to receive it.

Heavenly Father, we are so grateful for your presence in our lives and in this church. Help us to be who you have called us to be. Give us the wisdom to see it, the desire to engage it, and the courage to walk it out.

We are praying for our world, Father. We are aware of the recent court decision on abortion[2] and we are grateful for that decision. We believed the Roe v. Wade decision was a flawed decision to begin with. But at the same time we are leery, Father. We know that in actual practice not a whole lot is going to change as a result of this recent reversal, at least not in the short run. We know that both sides of the political divide will use it as a political weapon to attack the other side. So it will become even more divisive than it has been. We pray for you to use it for your purposes.

We pray for your wisdom to be with us and to be with all of your people and all of our leaders. Help us to see your truth and help us not to get caught up in needless conflicts but to honor your love and to care for your people and to manifest these fruits of the Spirit in our own lives.

So we pray for our leaders, Father, that you would give them wisdom. And we pray for you to use their decisions to accomplish your will and your purposes. And we know you will, you use our history to accomplish your purposes Father. We pray for mercy in the midst of it, mercy and grace, for we are a wayward people. We pray for your churches, Father.

Sometimes in the midst of the darkness that is growing, we get afraid that your churches are shrinking. It helps us to realize that the

2 https://en.wikipedia.org/wiki/Dobbs_v._Jackson_Women%27s_Health_Organization

darkness that is growing is part and parcel of the light that you are bringing to the world. As you bring your light to the world, you help us to see truth. And so we begin to see the world as it actually is, full of sin. And from your perspective it looks pretty dark, darker than we thought it was. So help us to understand that that vision of the world's darkness comes from you working in our lives and in the life of the world. You help us to see the world as it is, and it is full of sin.

So help us to be who you have called us to be here at St. Paul's. Help us to hold on to our faith, to be faithful. We continue to pray for all of your churches, those we like and those we don't like. We continue to pray that you would use them to accomplish your purposes. And we pray for you to guide us, to strengthen us, and to be with us as we know that you will.

In Jesus' name, amen.

June 26, 2022

The Road Ahead

"Rejoice with Jerusalem, and be glad for her, all you who love her; rejoice with her in joy, all you who mourn over her; 11 that you may nurse and be satisfied from her consoling breast; that you may drink deeply with delight from her glorious abundance." 12 For thus says the LORD: "Behold, I will extend peace to her like a river, and the glory of the nations like an overflowing stream; and you shall nurse, you shall be carried upon her hip, and bounced upon her knees. 13 As one whom his mother comforts, so I will comfort you; you shall be comforted in Jerusalem. 14 You shall see, and your heart shall rejoice; your bones shall flourish like the grass; and the hand of the LORD shall be known to his servants, and he shall show his indignation against his enemies. —*Isaiah 66:10-14*

Brothers, if anyone is caught in any transgression, you who are spiritual should restore him in a spirit of gentleness. Keep watch on yourself, lest you too be tempted. 2 Bear one another's burdens, and so fulfill the law of Christ. 3 For if anyone thinks he is something, when he is nothing, he deceives himself. 4 But let each one test his own work, and then his reason to boast will be in himself alone and not in his neighbor. 5 For each will have to bear his own load. 6 Let the one who is taught the word share all good things with the one who teaches. 7 Do not be deceived: God is not mocked, for whatever one sows, that will he also reap. 8 For the one who sows to his own flesh will from the flesh reap corruption, but the one who sows to the Spirit will from the Spirit reap eternal life. 9 And let us not grow weary of doing good, for in due season we will reap, if we do not give up. 10 So then, as we have opportunity, let us do good to everyone, and es-

pecially to those who are of the household of faith.

—Galatians 6:1-10

Isaiah's message of justice and hope for the future is a prediction of the eventual coming of Christ. He predicted that the coming of Christ would effect the whole world, believers and unbelievers alike. But the two groups would not be affected in the same ways because God treats believers differently than unbelievers.

We do the same thing in our courts. Law abiders are treated differently than law breakers. Both are confronted by the same laws, but they treat those laws differently. So, the court treats them differently. Law abiders are honored, and law breakers face punishment for their crimes. But again, both are judged by the same laws.

In the same way all people are effected by the coming of Christ. Christ's coming was a watershed event in history. The birth, death, and resurrection of Jesus Christ utterly changed the world. It even changed Judaism, in that after Christ animal sacrifices were abandoned by the Jews. The entire world was, is, and will be forever changed by Jesus Christ.

Paul wrote, "Brothers, if anyone is caught in any transgression, *you who are spiritual* should restore him in a spirit of gentleness." (Galatians 6:1). He acknowledged that those who had responded to Christ with love and commitment were different from those who did not so respond. However, contrary to popular opinion today, spirituality is not a privilege; rather, it imposes an obligation of faithful service to others. It is an obligation of restoration, an obligation to bring back to or put back into a former state or condition.

Paul was simply acknowledging the reality of sin in the world. Sin was and still is the current condition of the whole world. Original sin is the reality of the world. We are all born sinners, which means that we all must be changed in order to escape the consequences of sin. But before the world fell into sin following Adam (Genesis 3), the world—natural humanity—did not know sin. Their former condition, prior to God's judgment, was ignorance of sin. Thus, their former condition can be described as sinless in that they didn't know what sin was.

The major thrust of human history according to the Bible was that God created the world and that world reflected God's perfection. But the world, humanity—Adam and Eve, were drawn into sin by a sinful creature who had rejected God. And when Adam and Eve followed the advice and thinking of that creature, they became aware of their sin. And their sin was cultural, it involved more than just them as individuals. Thus, human culture following Adam and Eve was fundamentally and irretrievably sinful. After several millennia, God sent Jesus Christ into the world to redeem it from sin. Thus, the historical pattern of the Bible is: creation, fall, redemption.

Jesus Christ is responsible for the redemption. What we do as followers of Jesus Christ is to extend His forgiveness to the world. Christians now function as the body of Christ in the world, offering forgiveness and restoration to repentant sinners. So, the historical pattern following Jesus Christ is: original sin, forgiveness, repentance, restoration.

Paul went on to say, "Keep watch on yourself, *lest you too be tempted*" (Galatians 6:1). Tempted by what? We are not all tempted by the same sin. We are each tempted by different sins. We all have our own unique preferences and predilections that lead us to different sins. The sin of lust is not tempting to the greedy. Paul was not talking about this kind of sin here. Rather, he was talking to Christians who had responded to Christ, who were in the process of renouncing sin. All sin tempts us to do evil. But what evil was Paul talking about here?

He was talking about the refusal to forgive and restore others, to hold the sins of others in more contempt than one's own sins. Because Christ's mission is a mission of restoration, and Christians represent the body of Christ, it is a sin to withhold restoration from those who want it. Even when their first efforts of repentance are shallow and delusory. Repentance is not done once, but must be practiced continually because our disengagement from sin is gradual, two steps forward, and one back. This is simply the reality of the human condition. Jesus knows this and works with sinners as they grow into the grace and mercy He provides.

However, sinners must actually *want* to be forgiven, which means that they must acknowledge and confess their sin. Not just once, not twice, but continuously because our sinfulness is more ingrained that we first believe. It is more tenacious than is imagined. Sin has the power to transform itself again and again.

Thus, ongoing repentance, daily repentance, is needed. Sinners who do not confess and continue to discover and confess their ongoing sin are not forgiven. It is not that Christ withholds it, but that they will not accept forgiveness because they think they don't need it. Or they think they already have as much as they need. They discount the severity and tenacity of their sin, their self-deception, or justification of their sins.

Paul went on, "Bear one another's burdens, and so fulfill the law of Christ" (Galatians 6:2). To bear another's burdens means to put up with each other, to endure one another without complaint. These few words communicate a very big ask. It does not mean that Christians should tolerate whatever behavior people engage. We are not to tolerate sin, but neither are we to withhold mercy and forgiveness from sinners.

This simple idea has many far ranging implications. Christians are to both confess and forgive. So we find ourselves telling others our problems and listening to the personal problems of others. Both of these things are necessary. And part of the process is the identification of sin in our own lives and in the lives of others. We must help one another identify sin because people tend to be blind to their own sin.

There are various ways to do this. We can help one another by giving of our time, talent, and treasure. Note that this is not time, talent, *or* treasure, but time, talent, *and* treasure. We should be actively sharing all of these things. And when we can do nothing else, we can always pray for one another about various problems.

We always need to work on other people's problems *and* our own problems at the same time. "Bear one another's burdens… 5 bear his own load" (Galatians 6:2, 5). Sharing burdens does not absolve us from responsibility for ourselves. We must do both. Most of the time our problems are similar to the problems of others, and we can learn from one another by making application to ourselves. Sharing and receiving help is a two-way street.

Our Achilles's heel is self-deception. It's always easier to see the problems of others than to see our own. It usually takes someone else to point our our problems. And when others point out our problems it is difficult to receive and accept their analysis. We all tend to have inflated self-images. Paul said, "For if anyone thinks he is something, when he is nothing, he deceives himself" (Galatians 6:3). Thus we must always be ready to admit that self-deception or self-delusion is possible, even likely. Who truly understands himself?

In the past forty or so years people in American have decidedly gotten worse in terms of knowing ourselves. Why? Because our public schools have been teaching the importance of self-esteem. We have been taught to esteem ourselves. And while this can make us feel better, it also distorts our understanding of who and what we actually are. We are taught to discount our own liabilities and sins. Sins?! Yes, according to God all human beings are sinners from birth. The Bible calls it original sin (Genesis 3). To deny this historic reality is to deny something very important about ourselves, about our character. When the need for positive self-perception races ahead of reality, the likely result is a socially inept misfit who cannot deal with social criticism. If you are offended by the suggestion that you are a sinner, then you fall into this category.

As part of a decades-long study that has tracked 130 individuals since nursery school, a team of researchers assessed the subjects' personalities at ages 18 and 23, monitoring such traits as dependability and how subjects handle life's frustrations. The volunteers provided self-descriptions, and their friends contributed evaluations as well. When the researchers looked at subjects who were "self-enhancers"—those whose glowing self-image bore little resemblance to their true personality—a disturbing portrait emerged.

> "Self-enhancers tend to be hostile, lack social skills, and appear anxious and moody. They are sensitive to criticism and keep people at a distance—perhaps so that they don't get negative

> feedback that might alter their overly positive view. They are trying to hide their flaws from themselves."[3]

This is the result of forty years of public education that pushed self-esteem. When friends see through the facade, those who self-enhance engage in increasing distortion and denial in an attempt to maintain a positive self-view. Artificially propping up self-esteem may provide a temporary mental boost, but in the long run it stunts their social and personal well-being.

> *"Let the one who is taught the word share all good things with the one who teaches. Do not be deceived: God is not mocked, for whatever one sows, that will he also reap" (Galatians 6:6-7).*

Here we see that the teacher and the taught are in a reciprocal relationship where each shares his or her gifts with the other. We also see the idea of Karma, where intent and actions of an individual (cause) influence the future of that individual (effect). Reaping what you sow is a very old idea that is mostly true, but it is not absolute. It certainly applies to sinners in that sinners sow sin and reap sin as a reward or consequence. The biblical understanding of this idea is that sinners cannot overcome the consequences of sin on their own. Sinners will continue to sin because sin is natural to them, and they will reap the consequences of sin. Yet, this is not the whole truth according to the Bible.

The Bible also teaches about God's grace, and grace is different than Karma. Strictly speaking Karma applies to reincarnation within the Hindu construction of reality. Yet it is common to apply it to ordinary living in the sense that people get what they deserve. But the Bible also teaches that people get what they don't deserve. God's grace, God's mercy and forgiveness are freely given to people who do not deserve them. Nonetheless, the fact that God gives believers what they don't deserve—forgiveness—does not negate the consequences of our sowing and reaping.

God gives it freely, but what you do with it generates consequences. If you receive God's grace, then mercy and forgiveness are

---

3 https://www.psychologytoday.com/us/articles/199511/self-delusion-i-love-me

yours. But if you deny and/or neglect God's grace, if you do not willingly accept it, then you do not receive God's mercy and forgiveness, and you continue in your sin and its consequences.

> *"For the one who sows to his own flesh will from the flesh reap corruption, but the one who sows to the Spirit will from the Spirit reap eternal life" (Galatians 6:8).*

Another interesting thing about God's grace: it is not given *to* us, it is given *through* us. When you receive God's grace you become a member of Christ's body, the church. And God works through His church. God's grace does not fall randomly out of the sky. Rather, God works through His people, His body. God's people pass His grace and mercy forward to others. God gives us grace and we are to pass it forward. When we do, it creates more grace. But when we don't, it results in more sin. Of course, no one does this perfectly. We will fail, but our failure must not become a justification for giving up. God will not fail to complete what He has begun.

> *"So then, as we have opportunity, let us do good to everyone, and especially to those who are of the household of faith" (Galatians 6:10).*

God treats believers and unbelievers differently, and so do we. Our civil laws treat law abiders differently than law breakers. Those who abide by the law do not receive the consequences that are given to those who break the law. The law is supposed to treat everyone equally, the same. The law does not give special privileges to anyone. Nor should any privileges given by the law be withheld from anyone. All are supposed to be equal before the law. This is the basis of our equality. The same laws apply to all people in the same way. This is what justice is. This defines fairness. Justice or fairness does not provide the same result for everyone, it provides the same opportunity for everyone. The results or consequences of the law are different for those who do not break the law than for those who do break the law. Justice or fairness requires these different outcomes.

However, law and love are quite different. Where the law applies to everyone equally, love cannot apply to all equally. Love is a special affection, and when it applies to everyone equally, it actually applies to no one in particular because love requires *special* treatment. We don't love everyone the same. If you doubt this, ask your husband or wife if it is okay for you to love everyone in the same ways that s/he loves you. No! By definition love is particular, special. To love everyone equally means loving no one in particular.

And that is not the gospel! Christians are not called to love everyone the same. Nor to treat everyone the same. To treat everyone in the same ways undermines the special uniqueness of love. Love requires special regard.

But doesn't God love all people equally? He does because He is perfect. We don't because we are not. God loves everyone enough to give everyone the same law to guide them in this life. Thus, God's law (the Ten Commandments) apply equally to all people, for all time, and in all human cultures. And yet, God treats law abiders differently than He treats law breakers. However, because of original sin all people are born sinners, which means that God's curse falls on every individual.

We are all cursed from birth. However, a long time ago God sent Jesus Christ to undo that curse by granting mercy and forgiveness to repentant sinners. God's grace, God's gift of love, mercy, and forgiveness has been given to humanity as a whole, to all human beings. God's love has already been given to everyone for all time. That gift is a done deal!

Yet, the gift is not complete until it is received. Love blooms only when and where it is reciprocated. Love becomes perfect or whole only when it is both given and received. Unrequited love is tragic because it is not reciprocated. Unrequited love means love that is not reciprocated. When love is not mutual, each loving the other, it is not complete, not whole, not perfect.

God's love is perfect, which means that it comes into full bloom when it is received and returned. God loves everyone, but when people do not love God in return, their failure to love God in return means that their connection to God is hampered. And that particular expression of God's love, then, will not bloom. The deficiency is not in God, but in the one who does not return God's love. And the failure to return God's love issues from a failure to properly receive it. And not receiving God's love, which includes His grace, mercy, and forgiveness, means that people continue in their sin and will receive the consequences of their sin—damnation.

Thus, the gospel of Jesus Christ is that God loves humanity, including the ungodly. And God has given His love, His grace, His mercy, and His forgiveness to one and all equally through Jesus Christ. His love, having already been given, must be received and returned. The proverbial ball is in our court, in *your* court.

The purpose of God's love is not to celebrate us as we are, but to change us into His likeness. God loves us, warts and all. But He also loves us enough not to leave us as we are. Receiving God's love changes people. No one can respond to God's love without first becoming a different person, a Christ-like person. That's the mission of Jesus Christ.

Some will and some won't, but all are called. What about you? Are you willing?

July 3, 2022

Do Likewise

The LORD your God will make you abundantly prosperous in all the work of your hand, in the fruit of your womb and in the fruit of your cattle and in the fruit of your ground. For the LORD will again take delight in prospering you, as he took delight in your fathers, 10 when you obey the voice of the LORD your God, to keep his commandments and his statutes that are written in this Book of the Law, when you turn to the LORD your God with all your heart and with all your soul. 11 "For this commandment that I command you today is not too hard for you, neither is it far off. 12 It is not in heaven, that you should say, 'Who will ascend to heaven for us and bring it to us, that we may hear it and do it?' 13 Neither is it beyond the sea, that you should say, 'Who will go over the sea for us and bring it to us, that we may hear it and do it?' 14 But the word is very near you. It is in your mouth and in your heart, so that you can do it.

—Deuteronomy 30:9-14

25 And behold, a lawyer stood up to put him to the test, saying, "Teacher, what shall I do to inherit eternal life?" 26 He said to him, "What is written in the Law? How do you read it?" 27 And he answered, "You shall love the Lord your God with all your heart and with all your soul and with all your strength and with all your mind, and your neighbor as yourself." 28 And he said to him, "You have answered correctly; do this, and you will live." 29 But he, desiring to justify himself, said to Jesus, "And who is my neighbor?" 30 Jesus replied, "A man was going down from Jerusalem to Jericho, and he fell among robbers, who stripped him and beat him and departed, leaving him half dead. 31 Now by chance a priest was going down that road, and when he saw him he passed by on the other side. 32 So likewise a Levite, when he came to the place and saw him, passed by on the other side. 33 But a Samaritan, as he journeyed, came to where he was, and when he saw him, he had compassion. 34 He went to him and bound up his wounds, pouring on oil and wine. Then he set him on his own animal and brought him to an inn and took care of him. 35 And the next day he took out two denari and gave them to the innkeeper, saying, 'Take care of him, and whatever more you spend, I will repay you when I come back.' 36 Which of these three, do you think, proved to be a neighbor to the man who fell among the robbers?" 37 He said, "The one who showed him mercy." And Jesus said to him, "You go, and do likewise." —*Luke 10:25-37*

The first part of the scripture reading comes out of Deuteronomy 30. And there we learn that prosperity is the result of faithfulness. That's what the Lord is teaching. If we will be faithful, the Lord will prosper us. That doesn't necessarily mean that God will make us rich. There is more to prosperity than money. He also says that faithfulness is possible. It was possible for the ancient Israelites to be faithful.

And yet in the Scripture as we read through the Old Testament we see that Israel was not faithful over the centuries. Israel continually fell into faithlessness and disrepute. And so the larger biblical issue here really is how could Israel become faithful? Faithfulness of God's people is what the Bible is aiming at. How can people become faithful? How can *we* become faithful?

The larger lesson that the Old Testament teaches is that real faithfulness, perfect faithfulness, is impossible, which is difficult to hear. But the truth is that faithfulness is impossible without a change of heart and mind. Scripture tells us that God can and does change hearts and minds. He's done that to many people over many centuries. God does change hearts and minds! But in addition to that, or as a consequence of that, people still need to actually be faithful. God changes our hearts and minds, but we still need to walk the walk. A changed heart puts us on the path of faithfulness, but we still need to walk the path. We still need to do the work of faithfulness. There is more to attaining a thing than simply wanting it.

Wanting it is necessary. It's the first leg of the journey. But the actual journey must still be traversed.

The second scripture from Luke speaks to this issue. A lawyer came to test Jesus. It would be a lawyer, wouldn't it? Lawyers are a particular breed. They are a function of their education. So they ask legal questions. And if you look carefully at what the lawyer asked, you will see that he did not ask: *how can I be saved?* That's not what he said. Lawyers are very careful with their words. He said, "What shall I do to inherit eternal life?" (Luke 10:25).

He asked a legal question, a behavioral question. What was the nature of his legal question? Inheritance. Inheritance is a legal term. To inherit something is to receive a property or a right or a title by succession, or perhaps through a last will and testament. The interesting thing about inheritance is that if I'm going to receive an inheritance, my decision has nothing to do with it. It's the decision of somebody else that determines my inheritance. It's the decision of whoever owns whatever it is that they're passing on. They decide who is going to get it. Not the guy who gets it. So in that sense, inheritance always comes as a gift.

When Jesus was asked this question, He turned to the law. He said, *What does the law say? What is written there?* The lawyer knew the law, the Scripture, and he repeated it. He understood what it said. And he understood it correctly. So Jesus said, *Okay. You know what to do. Do that.*

But Luke said that the lawyer wanted to justify himself. He had asked the question in order to justify himself. What does it mean for people to justify themselves? Self-justification describes how, when a person encounters cognitive dissonance, or a situation in which a person's behavior is inconsistent with their beliefs (hypocrisy), that person tends to justify the behavior and deny any negative feedback associated with the behavior. Self-justification is the attempt to justify our actions and decisions, especially the ones inconsistent with our beliefs. It comes from the unpleasant feeling called cognitive dissonance, when we realize that our actions are not in line with our beliefs. It's a kind of hypocrisy.

The lawyer wanted to justify his own behavior, and to deny any negative feedback associated with his behavior. Self-justification is a moral issue and it comes into play when our morality sets a certain bar, when we realize that we have crossed a line we should not have crossed. It comes into play whether we officially ascribe to it or not. A lot of social morality is simply absorbed unconsciously.

Our sense of morality tells us what is expected of us in this or that situation. And we get justification when we meet those moral expectations. If we can do what the law calls us to do, then we're justified. At lease we feel justified. We feel good about ourselves.

There are two classic ways that people can justify themselves. We can improve our performance and meet the bar, meet those expectations. Or we can lower the bar, lower the expectations. And if we lower the bar, then we have met the bar, so we feel justified. Self-justification is often a matter of lowering the bar.

Again, the need to justify our actions and decisions, especially the ones that are inconsistent with our beliefs, comes from the unpleasant feeling called *cognitive dissonance* or *hypocrisy*. And when that feeling of cognitive dissonance sinks into us we realize we might be guilty of hypocrisy. And nobody wants to feel that. So we need to make a behavioral adjustment. We either improve our behavior, or we lower the bar. Those are the two alternatives we have.

The lawyer asks, *Who is my neighbor?* Loving God for the lawyer did not present a problem, or so he said. But loving his neighbor presented a problem. Loving God is easy, or we can make it easy. If we believe in our own idea of God, then loving God is pretty easy because we are just loving our own idea of God. It's a function of self-love. But loving people, loving sinners is a lot more difficult. People are quirky. People stink, and sometimes they bite.

The question that the lawyer asked suggests that there were some people who might not be his neighbor. So he could feel okay about not loving them. That's what he was trying to say. So the question that he asked revealed a false understanding of God's law. He was interpreting God's law to suit himself. And when he asked the question Jesus told him a story. Why wouldn't Jesus just simply answer the question. He could have, but He didn't. He told this particular story, a parable. A parable is a story that has a moral lesson to it.

What we learn from Jesus not answering the question directly but giving the man a story to think about, is that Jesus knew that when people ask questions, especially questions like that, they don't really want an answer. If you give them an answer, your answer will probably not work for them because any answer you give them is *your* answer, not *their* answer. Providing a parable, a moral lesson is more effective because it forces people to answer their own questions.

If you've ever been involved in counseling, psychological counseling, or any kind of counseling, you will notice that that is exactly what counselors do. Counselors don't tell their clients what to do. They don't answer their questions. They just keep people talking until they figure it out for themselves. That is the only way it works because when you figure it out for yourself, you have *your* answer. That is what Jesus was doing.

What was the story that Jesus told? There was this guy from Jerusalem. And that's an important point. The guy is traveling from Jerusalem. The implication is that this fellow who was traveling was from Jerusalem. He was a Jew, not a Samaritan. This important detail will come into play shortly. So, this Jew from Jerusalem gets beaten up and robbed on the highway.

It happened on a notoriously dangerous road probably at night. The traveler was kind of dumb for being on that road in the first place, and being on it at night was even dumber. The traveler who was robbed appears to be an undiscerning dummy. This detail provides an unflattering assessment of Jews in general. This is the setup: the guy gets robbed and beat up and left for dead on the side of the road. He's a dumb guy who did a dumb thing, and he is a Jew.

So a priest comes across him, and that's important because the priest is a priest of the Jewish people. He ought to have some compassion for the beaten man. There were two categories of priests in the Old Testament. There were the Aaronites, the sons of Aaron, and the Levites, the sons of Levi. The Aaronites were similar to what we would call elders. The Aaronites were charged with Temple worship. They did all the stuff regarding worship. Back in those days they didn't have just candles to light. They had to sacrifice animals, which required both set up and clean up. It was a big deal, a lot of work.

Because the priest was an Aaronite he might have thought that the situation on the road was out of his responsibility. Caring for the guy wasn't the kind of the thing that he as a priest was charged to do. So he might have thought that a Levite priest would be better suited to take care of him because that was their responsibility. The Levitical priests were responsible for caring for the poor. The Aaronic priest may have though, *It's not my job*. So he passed by on the other side of the road.

Then a Levitical priest came along. The Levitical priest is kind of like our Deacons in a sense. The Deacons are not charged with administering worship, they are charged with all of the other stuff: Taking care of the building and the grounds, and the money, the purse. And in ancient Israel they were also in charge of what we would call *charity* or *alms*. The Temple collected money, and it was up to the Levitical priests to distribute it to the poor, to those in need, etc. That was their job. The first priest knew these classifications and the different priestly jobs, and likely thought, *That's not my job. That's the other priest's job.* And passed him by. He probably had an important meeting to get to.

Next the Levite came across him, and the Levite should know better. Helping this man was the job of the Levite. He might even have recognized the guy on the side of the road. But he might have known that this guy was not a member of his congregation. Jerusalem would have been much smaller than it is now. So he might have known everybody who was a Jew. But he didn't know this guy. So he might conclude that this guy wasn't a Jew. He wasn't a member of a synagogue that he knew. And so he also passed by on the other side of the road. The Levi passed by on the other side of the road.

The story continued with a Samaritan who came across him. The Samaritans and the Jews were arch enemies. They had a long-term rivalry, worse than some of the football, baseball, or basketball rivalries that we have in our day. The Samaritans hated the Jews and the Jews hated the Samaritans because hundreds of years ago when Israel was sacked, way back in 700 B.C. Syria carted off the the Jewish intelligentsia to make them slaves. The Jewish people who were of the upper class, who were controlling things, those who had money and education, were removed from Jerusalem and made slaves of the Assyrians. They took them off to Assyria to become part of their empire because those people would be useful. They left all the blue collar workers, the country bumpkins, in Samaria, which was in the country north of Jerusalem.

And because the Jerusalem Temple was destroyed, sacrifices could not be performed there. The people in Samaria wanted to continue being Jewish, so they established their own temple in Samaria, and did their best to reproduce all of the details of temple activity. Eventually they created their own temple, and they believed in the first five books of the Old Testament. But that's all they had. Over the centuries the Samaritan religious practices grew, and eventually they had their own temple and their own priests. They did their own thing, not in association with Jerusalem. They were separate from the Jerusalem Temple, even when it had been rebuilt. And that set up this conflict between the Samaritan worship practice and the Jerusalem worship practice. So, Jerusalem Jews hated Samaritan Jews, and Samaritan Jews hated Jerusalem Jews. Each side thought that the other side were doing it wrong. Each accused the other of false worship.

So in the story a Samaritan comes across a Jew, that's an important detail. In all likelihood this lawyer who has been listening to the story would himself think that no help could be given to or received from a Samaritan. Jews wouldn't have anything to do with Samaritans. They thought that there was no such thing as a "*good* Samaritan." But in this story the Samaritan had compassion and took care of the Jew at great expense to himself. He paid for the doctor and the food and the lodging and the care, and then promised to cover *all* expenses. This was not a not a cheap fix. The guy threw some serious money at it.

There is moral lessons to this parable. One of the moral lessons we need to learn is that our expectations about people, especially about people we don't personally know very well, are likely to be wrong. Whatever we think about them—good or bad—is more than likely going to be wrong. Another lesson is that our neighbors include everyone around us. A neighbor is anybody who is in your orbit, in your area of influence, in your social circle, not simply in your neighborhood. Your neighbor is anybody that you come in contact with, long term or short. They become a neighbor when they get near you.

The central lesson is that we are to love those who are near us. We are to give help and share the gospel with anyone we come in contact with. But this does not necessarily suggest that everybody is going to get saved. Some people tend to jump to that conclusion because Jesus said that we are to love our enemies. If we love our neighbors and our enemies that would include most everybody in the world. The lesson is not that everyone is already saved, or will be saved, or should be saved. That's not what this story means.

We are to love our enemies, but we are not to agree with or to promote the enemy's false perspective. We can love people without agreeing with them. We can love people and still understand them to be wrong, even hell-bound. We can love them. We can offer them grace and mercy and help. And, in fact, we should do that because the grace and mercy that we extend to them becomes an act of evangelism. And when mercy or grace is given as an act of evangelism, it must include the gospel of Jesus Christ. If it doesn't include the gospel, then it's not an act of evangelism. Mercy becomes an act of evangelism only when it includes the gospel.

> *"But He answered and said, 'It is written, "Man shall not live on bread alone, but on every word that proceeds out of the mouth of God"' (Matthew 4:4).*

This means that the gospel is more important than food. Food will sustain life, but only the gospel will sustain eternal life. So when we are gracious and merciful to people who are in need, we should share the gospel with them. It doesn't mean we need to beat them over the head with it. It just means that we need to acknowledge the reality of Jesus Christ.

In this story the lawyer's concern was to exclude some people from the mercy of neighborliness, which, if we understand neighborliness as an extension of evangelism, would exclude them from the gospel, as well. So Jesus' concern was for all people to be merciful to one another as a way to share the gospel with everyone. And whether people receive the gospel, whether they act upon the gospel is not up to us. That's not our call. That belongs to the Lord. However, we are to simply share what we know about Jesus Christ.

The problem is that our preconceptions about people often get in the way of God's love. What we think about people affects how we treat them. But when we err in this regard, we should always err on the side of grace and mercy. We should always be gracious and merciful to everyone, even when it will cost us, even when there might be harm that comes to us. We should not withhold the gospel from anyone. That's what Jesus did. He is our model, and harm came to Him.

The lesson of this story, this parable, hits us right between the eyes. In a sense, Jesus is saying, not only to the lawyer but to all of His people, to all the world: *Can you love your enemies? Can you love those who oppose the gospel without omitting the gospel from our love for them?* This is a huge issue in today's world because there are lots of people opposed to the gospel. Lots of people think that if you don't *agree* with them, then you don't *love* them. And that is simply not true.

How can we love people with whom we disagree? Jesus suggests that the best thing we can do is love them enough to tell them the truth, the whole truth as best we understand it. And as the people of God we understand that the Truth is a Person, not a statement, not an idea, not a program. His name is Jesus! We are to listen to everyone and be gracious and merciful to them. We are to help them understand that we are acting as the hands and feet of Jesus. We are showing God's love to them. Scripture says that we are to love God *and* neighbor.

That reminds me of Gandhi. He would say, *I love your Jesus, but I don't care for your Christians*. It's an interesting perspective, and an awful lot of people have that perspective. We need to work on that! Can *you* help with that?

Heavenly Father, we are so grateful that you are with us and have led us and guided us. We thank you for your leadership and your guidance. We thank you for your presence with this church for more than a century. And again, we pray that you would help us to be who you have called us to be. Give us the wisdom to understand it, the humility to accept it, and the courage to walk it out in the midst of these strange days in which we live.

We pray for those who are ill and infirm and unable to be with us this morning, for those who need your healing and your comfort. Be with us as we lift them up in the silence of our own thoughts. ... We pray blessings upon them. We pray for all of your people in all of your churches.

We pray for those who are neighbors to us, to this church, in our own town. We lift up all of your people and all of your pastors. We pray for the ones we like, and we even pray for the ones we don't like. We pray for them all to be faithful. We pray that you would help them to be who you have called them to be, just like you are helping us to be who you have called us to be.

We pray for an outpouring of your grace and your mercy the world over. We pray for the leaders of our world. We pray for local leaders and political leaders and religious leaders and educational leaders and medical leaders and business leaders, all of them. Father, we pray that you would make them supple to your Word and your way. Help them, help us all, to see the truth of your Word and its value in our lives and in our culture.

And help us to love you enough to be obedient, to find ways, to engage your Word in our own lives, in our world, in our prayers, in our neighborhoods, in our homes, at work, at school, at play—wherever we happen to be.

We are aware that war is raging. We are also aware that the twentieth century has been the most war-torn century in the history of the world. It's hard to believe because things seem relatively peaceful here, but there have been more wars in the last couple hundred years than ever before. So we pray against that spirit of war. We pray for those who are suffering in the midst of it, especially in Ukraine and elsewhere. We pray against those who are causing it, or leading it, or promoting it. And we pray that you would provide a fix that is in line with the ministry of Jesus Christ.

We know that you are doing that in the long run. Sometimes it is hard for us to see how all of your promises are going to work out, but it's not important that we understand *how* it's going to work out. It's important that we trust that *you* will work it out. So we pray for all of this, Father, and trust that that is exactly what you are doing. Have mercy in the midst of all of this. And again, help us to be who you have called us to be to. Help us to be your hands and your feet in little ways here and there, as best we are able. Amen.

July 10, 2022

The Good Portion

Why do you boast of evil, O mighty man? The steadfast love of God endures all the day. 2 Your tongue plots destruction, like a sharp razor, you worker of deceit. 3 You love evil more than good, and lying more than speaking what is right. Selah! 4 You love all words that devour, O deceitful tongue. 5 But God will break you down forever; he will snatch and tear you from your tent; he will uproot you from the land of the living. Selah! 6 The righteous shall see and fear, and shall laugh at him, saying, 7 "See the man who would not make God his refuge, but trusted in the abundance of his riches and sought refuge in his own destruction!" 8 But I am like a green olive tree in the house of God. I trust in the steadfast love of God forever and ever. 9 I will thank you forever, because you have done it. I will wait for your name, for it is good, in the presence of the godly.

—Psalm 52:1-9

38 Now as they went on their way, Jesus entered a village. And a woman named Martha welcomed him into her house. 39 And she had a sister called Mary, who sat at the Lord's feet and listened to his teaching. 40 But Martha was distracted with much serving. And she went up to him and said, "Lord, do you not care that my sister has left me to serve alone? Tell her then to help me." 41 But the Lord answered her, "Martha, Martha, you are anxious and troubled about many things, 42 but one thing is necessary. Mary has chosen the good portion, which will not be taken away from her." —Luke 10:38-42

Psalm 52 is really about God's care for His faithful people, especially when they're surrounded by God's enemies. This seems very appropriate in today's world. At least it seems so to me, because Christians are again surrounded by God's enemies today. There is a reality of evil that we don't like to recognize, but we must recognize it because it's true. That reality is that people generally love what God calls evil, and they boast of it because it actually conforms almost perfectly to their own desires and beliefs. Evil conforms to the desires and beliefs of Godlessness.

Godless people don't think of what they think or say or do as evil, they think of them as part of their own personal integrity, their own personal authenticity. They see their own desires and beliefs as elements of their own personal truth. They embrace the things that God calls evil. But in reality they don't own such things. Such things owns them.

People today don't really seem to know or care about biblical truth. They don't know about God's truth or real truth. And the reason that they don't know or care about God's truth is that they are never exposed to it in today's world. It's not part of their home life. They don't see it or learn about it in school, or on television, or in the media. They're not reading their Bibles, if they have one. And they're not exposed to it at church because they're not going to church, most of them. And when they do, too few churches preach and teach God's truth today. To many churches and pastors are content with telling stories and keeping their people content—passive. No one wants a discontented church, a church that fights and bickers.

Because people don't know God's stories, God's values, God's truth, they don't value what they don't know. This describes most people in the world today. But before we judge them too harshly we need to realize that we were all like that at one point in our lives, all of us, every one of us. Before we became Christians, before we learned about God, we too didn't value what God values. So it's silly for us to expect people to value something that they don't know. It just isn't going to happen. Our job then, as Christians, is to do what we can to expose people to biblical truth.

We need to expose the reality of biblical truth to the world, to people who don't know Christ personally, intimately. We need to proclaim God's truth, lift it up, talk about it, teach it, wherever we can. And where we can't, we need to find a way. Our obligation is to witness and to share God's truth, to witness and to share God's stories as best as we are able, as best we can understand it. Nobody will do it perfectly, and it doesn't have to be done perfectly. If it's done perfectly, thoroughly, too much too soon, it puts people off. People need a chance to grow into it, to adapt themselves to it. Because it's challenging, confronting, even threatening. God's truth threatens to destroy evil, to rid the world of it. So our witnessing is better if it isn't done perfectly right away.

Yet, the truth of the matter is that we can't change anybody's heart. We can't change anybody's mind. We can't even change our own minds. Have you ever tried to break a long established habit? That's what we're talking about. If you ever tried to do that, tried to change someone's mind about God, you know how true this is. We can't change people's hearts and minds. But God can. And God does.

The way he does that is by exposing people to His story, to history, to Bible stories. The Bible is a very big book, full of lots of complex and subtle stories. It takes a long time to digest the stories in the Bible, a long time to understand God, to see what it is that He is doing in this world. And the way He does that is He writes people who read His story into His story. Those who read about God and understand what they are reading, find it compelling, even irresistible. They find themselves in the stories, as if God is speaking about them and to them at times.

In other words, His story becomes compelling. It grabs you and calls you by name. It has a kind of natural, maybe even supernatural, sense of compulsion. It draws us in. It puts us into the story. And that way then God's story becomes our story. In the midst of all of that, because His story becomes our story, because we find ourselves in God's story, His story becomes true. As it becomes our own story, we begin to see it as true history.

As this happens, it becomes a calling. When we see ourselves in God's story, we find a role to play in His story. That role is our calling. Everyone has a particular role to play in the long history of

God's story in this world. However, our role is not likely to be a big role. Very few people have big roles. And we should be thankful we don't have a very big role, actually. Because a big role in God's story means a big sacrifice. Playing a role in God's story is costly. For most Christians, ordinary Christians who have a small role to play find that the cost is manageable.

In addition, everyone's calling in this grand story that God is writing, that God continues to write, is absolutely unique. Every role, no matter how large or small, is absolutely precious. Every role is valuable to the whole story. The little roles are actually more important than the large roles because more people have small roles than large roles. Christianity is aimed at the ordinary person.

The great Christians of history are great, don't get me wrong. But emulating greatness is difficult. It's fine for those who can do it. But most people aren't going to be great. Most people are ordinary, so emulating ordinary Christianity is more important because it is more doable by more people. God wants everyone to be like Jesus. In other words, the whole story won't be complete until the whole world realizes the value of Jesus Christ, until everyone makes Christ real in their ordinary lives. It won't be complete unless and until *your* part of that story is engaged and acted out as part of God's story.

To be faithful then we must trust in the steadfast love of God forever and always, even in the midst of struggle and difficulty. Even, as Psalm 52 was talking about, when we are surrounded by enemies. We need to trust God especially when we are surrounded by enemies. That is when we most need to trust in God's steadfast love. We especially need to trust God when we are in the midst of trouble.

Being faithful means being thankful in the midst of all things, all circumstances, both good and bad. We need to always be thankful to God. Faithfulness is thankfulness. And so Psalm 52:9 says, "I will wait for your name, for it is good, in the presence of the godly." I will wait for your *name*. There may be some translation issues here because it doesn't make a whole lot of sense. What does it mean to wait for His *name*? Wait for *Him*, I understand. Yet, when God calls us to wait, He doesn't mean that we should sit around like we're waiting for a bus. Doing nothing.

Rather, He means that we should be actively involved, like a waiter or a waitress *waits* a table. When a waitress or a waiter waits a table, what are they doing? They're anticipating the needs of everybody at the table, and supplying those needs. This is what waiting for God is all about. To wait means to serve, to anticipate the needs of others, and to supply those needs. That's what a waiter does.

We are to wait for God's *name*. Whenever we see a reference to the name of God, whenever we hear the phrase "the *name* of God," we should think of it as the "*character* of God." In the Old Testament and in old times generally, names were much more significant than they are today. In the old days, the name of a person emphasized or was an example of the character of the person. The Smiths shod horses and worked with iron. The Porters were people who carried baggage. You get the idea.

So, in the Bible, when we read about God's *name*, we should think of God's *character* because His name is about His character. When the Bible says that God's name is powerful, it doesn't meant that the word *God* is some kind of talisman, like *abracadabra*. It means that God's character is powerful.

So, when the Psalmist says, "I will wait for your name," he means that he will serve the character of God in that situation. He will anticipate God's needs and supply them as best as he is able. It means that he will rely on the character of God. And he will do that by practicing the character qualities of God; for us, the character qualities of Jesus Christ. He will imitate Christ's character. Thus, as we engage in our service to the Lord, let us be an example of His character. To serve the character of God means to personally manifest the character of Jesus Christ in your own life; as best as you are able, it fits and starts, two steps forward, one step back. We won't do it perfectly, but we should practice the character qualities of Jesus Christ everywhere and in all circumstances to the best of our abilities. We are to do it in the company of the godly and in the company of the ungodly, this is what faithfulness is all about.

The second part of our scripture reading from Luke 10 is the story of Mary and Martha, which is a familiar story. But I want to put it in its proper context this morning because so often when we hear this story, like we hear so many stories in the Bible, we pull them out of their context, and think that they are just an independent unit. But they're not. This story fits into the the larger story that Jesus is talking about. And it's very interesting.

Notice that the Mary and Martha's story follows immediately upon the good Samaritan story from the previous chapter. The good Samaritan story answered the question of the lawyer, who asked, *what must I do to be saved?* Jesus said, *the Scripture tells us to love God and our neighbor.* The lesson of the Good Samaritan story is about service to others, to our neighbors. The Good Samaritan is concerned with his *neighbor*. All of these stories fit together, they're not independent pieces. They are all part of the larger story of Jesus.

This lawyer asked, *what must I do to be saved?* Jesus said we must love God and our neighbors. The Good Samaritan was about loving a *neighbor*. The Mary and Martha story is about loving *God*. This story about Mary and Martha is about the other half of Jesus' answer to the rich young ruler. It's about loving God.

Of course, the Mary and Martha story is also about service. We find Martha very much involved in service. She and Mary are loving their neighbors as best they can, cooking, cleaning, helping. But Martha is doing it too hard. She was so caught up with her service to others that she was becoming frustrated, angry.

When we see this as part of the larger story we find that Jesus is still answering the issue raised by the rich, young ruler about loving God and neighbors. What does it mean to serve God and His people? There are two kinds of service involved in this story about Mary and Martha. Martha was serving God's people, serving her neighbors. And in this story Mary was serving God. By attending to Jesus, by listening to Jesus, Mary was also serving God's purpose. And that is the point of the Mary and Martha story.

In the first part of the larger story, the story of the good Samaritan, we find an example of how to serve your neighbor. The story of Mary and Martha provides an example of how to serve God. It was Mary in contrast to Martha who provides the example of service to God. Of course, both of these kinds of service are necessary. We are called to love God *and* to love our neighbors, to *both* serve God *and* serve our neighbors.

But we can easily get so caught up in one or the other kind of service that we deny or ignore the other kind. We can get so focused on loving God that we find ourselves no longer serving our neighbors. Or we can get so focused on serving our neighbors that we find ourselves no longer serving God. Both of those are wrong approaches or wrong solutions to the problem because both of these things, loving God and loving neighbors, are necessary. The story of Mary and Martha tells us that neither of these things should be neglected.

One other detail is that the story is actually about Martha and Mary *and Lazarus*. Here are a few additional thoughts about that story. First, it's about these three siblings living together in one household. There is no mention of parents, so we will assume that the parents have died. There is no mention of any spouses, either. So the scholars assume that all three of them were single. That's interesting. It was an unusual household, or perhaps the three of them were very young.

Also in that culture, in the New Testament culture, it was traditional that men had certain jobs and women had certain jobs. The traditional understanding was that the women served the men in that culture, especially around food and household chores. So given these additional details, we find that Mary broke that rule. She wasn't serving. She was sitting at Jesus' feet, listening. Again, that's interesting because it would have been unusual. We also see that Jesus ignored the old tradition, that suggested that Mary should be in the kitchen helping, and He encouraged Mary to grow spiritually. In that culture, spiritual growth was for men, not women. Men studied the Scripture, women worked at home.

And we find that Martha demanded that Mary maintain the traditional role of women. Martha complained to Jesus, "Lord, do you not care that my sister has left me to serve alone? Tell her then to help me" (Luke 10:40). *Get her to help me! She's not doing her job! You need to tell her, Jesus!*

Jesus disagreed. That's interesting because He now voiced His disagreement with tradition. Of course, Martha's role was important. Jesus was not saying that service to others is an unimportant role. And He didn't invite Martha to sit down with Mary because this story was providing a contrast between the sisters. Martha's service needed to happen. Jesus' point was that service to others is good, but not adequate. It's not enough. We could argue the same thing on the other side. Serving God is not enough either. We must include serving our neighbors. Both are essential.

Jesus did not favor male roles over female roles in society, nor did he favor female roles over male roles in society. Rather, what He was saying was that everybody needs to do both of these things. Love God. Love your neighbors. Serve God and serve your neighbor.

Martha had been operating from the wrong motivation. She was very full of herself. She wasn't really meeting the needs of the people. She was busy complaining to Jesus. She was very full of herself. And because she was full of herself, she was distracted from her service. Martha was irritated with Mary, who was not helping. Martha became kind of snappy because she was self-concerned. Her self-concern, her complaining, kept her from both kinds of service. She stopped serving others to complain about Mary; and she was not engaged in service to Jesus, either. She was not listening to Jesus.

Hospitality and generosity are good things. They are signs of God's kingdom, and we need to honor those kinds of things. So Martha was not wrong in serving others. But her attitude about it was wrong. How she was going about it was wrong. Because she was self-concerned; she was likely jealous of Mary or angry with Mary.

On the other side of it, Mary was not wrong for neglecting her service duties. Rather, she was in service to God, which from her perspective at that point, was a higher calling, a higher duty. In the story Mary represents the idea that women also need spiritual growth, women also need to have a personal relationship with Jesus.

And Jesus honored that because God comes first. But because God comes first, that doesn't mean that service to others can be avoided. We all must do both.

So together these two sisters, Martha and Mary, embody the truth that generosity or love of neighbor and love of God are intertwined realities. We must always hold them together. We are not to choose between Martha and Mary. We are not to get mad at Martha or Mary for whatever reasons, because each one was denying something that the other was involved in. But rather both are to be honored.

Jesus was not denouncing the traditional roles of men and women. Both roles are important, serve God and serve others. Jesus was saying that both men and women needed to be doing both of those things. The gospel is far more important, far more valuable than our traditional roles.

We too often get caught up in traditional roles, and neglect other things that are also important. We just fall into our traditional roles without thinking about them. And this story calls us to think more deeply about these things. Those roles, the things we do in service to God and service to others, are important. Neither can be neglected, and we all need to be engaged in both of these things.

But in the midst of all of that, we also need to remember that God is to be our first priority. God is first. Otherwise, our service to our neighbors will likely be wrongly motivated. If we don't keep God first, our motivations for everything else will be faulty.

We are not to choose between Mary and Martha, but to honor them both. We are to honor the roles of both, and we all should be engaged in both of those roles all the time.

Heavenly Father, again, we are so blessed to be in your presence, to be able to come to church, and to worship you as we choose, as you call us. We give you thanks and praise for that. We give you thanks and praise for this church and her long history. We give you thanks for the people that are here, and for those with whom we minister.

We pray for this world, Father, this sin-soaked world in which we live. We are concerned about the world, concerned that it does not seem to be following your way and yet we know you are sovereign. We know that you are in control of all things. So help us to know that you are working out your truth in this world in a way that will honor the ministry of Jesus Christ.

Help us to be on the right side of history, on the right side of your story, Father. As you have written us into your story, give us wisdom and courage to act out our role, to play our role, to be who you have called us to be in the situations that you have given us. Some of those situations seem to us to be difficult, and so we pray for the strength to endure them in terms of our leaders and struggles in the world.

Father, we pray for those who are for you and against those who are against you, not against them personally, but against decisions and policies and actions that are not in line with your Word and your truth. So we are praying for your kingdom to manifest, Father. We know that we can't bring it in, and yet we also know that it won't be completed until we are in it.

And so help us, Father, give us wisdom and courage. Help us to simply be faithful and to lift up simple faithfulness in this world as a beacon of light. Make it so, Father. Amen.

Double Vision

*God has taken his place in the divine council; in the midst of the gods
he holds judgment: 2 "How long will you judge unjustly and show
partiality to the wicked? Selah 3 Give justice to the weak and the fa-
therless; maintain the right of the afflicted and the destitute. 4 Rescue
the weak and the needy; deliver them from the hand of the wicked." 5
They have neither knowledge nor understanding, they walk about in
darkness; all the foundations of the earth are shaken. 6 I said, "You
are gods, sons of the Most High, all of you; 7 nevertheless, like men
you shall die, and fall like any prince." 8 Arise, O God, judge the
earth; for you shall inherit all the nations! —Psalm 82*

*49 "I came to cast fire on the earth, and would that it were already
kindled! 50 I have a baptism to be baptized with, and how great is
my distress until it is accomplished! 51 Do you think that I have
come to give peace on earth? No, I tell you, but rather division. 52
For from now on in one house there will be five divided, three against
two and two against three. 53 They will be divided, father against
son and son against father, mother against daughter and daughter
against mother, mother-in-law against her daughter-in-law and
daughter-in-law against mother-in-law." 54 He also said to the
crowds, "When you see a cloud rising in the west, you say at once, 'A
shower is coming.' And so it happens. 55 And when you see the
south wind blowing, you say, 'There will be scorching heat,' and it
happens. 56 You hypocrites! You know how to interpret the appear-
ance of earth and sky, but why do you not know how to interpret the
present time? —Luke 12:49-56*

The lectionary is giving us some challenging material. This is another one of those tough messages. I want you to know that I didn't choose this topic, not really. It was given to me by the lectionary. It's in the Bible, and I will do my best to explain it.

Lord, cover me with your blessing and grace as we launch into this material. Help it to bless those who hear your Word. Give me the words, in Jesus name. Amen.

As you know, God's Word applies to us living today though it was written a long time ago. The preaching of God's Word applies to God's people, to all who hear His Word. God's Word applies to all sorts of people in all sorts of cultures in all sorts of situations in every period of time. The primary quality of God's Word is that it has many applications—even universal application. It applies in different ways to all people in every time and in all circumstances.

And so my preaching has application this morning for us who are gathered here today. But if it doesn't reach beyond these walls, it will fail to honor God's Word. You see, the renewal that we seek for St. Paul's is really more than the renewal of St. Paul's. If we are only focused on renewing our own church, we are self-focused. And that is not what the gospel is. The gospel is not self-focused. The gospel is other-focused. Love is other-focused.

Our concern as a church also needs to be other-focused because that is the purpose of God's Word. The goal of Christian preaching, the goal of Christian ministry, is the renewal of the whole world. It is not something that pastors can do, but it is what God is doing with His people. Fortunately, God says that His strength shines in us best through our weakness. In other words, when we are strong, we are full of ourselves, and we tend to ignore God's presence. But when we are weak then His truth can shine through us all the better.

So we are in luck, in God's grace actually, because we are weak. I am a weak reed sounding God's advance. Praise be to God! We offer our weakness this morning. Bear with me.

Psalm 82 sets up Luke 12. Psalm 82 tells us that wickedness in this world is a reality. There are people who walk about in darkness, people who love darkness. And that wickedness and darkness generally opposes God's people. We see this in the traditional Christmas readings.

> *"The people who walked in darkness have seen a great light; those who lived in a land of deep darkness on them light has shined" (Isaiah 9:2).*

> *"And this is the judgment: the light has come into the world, and people loved the darkness rather than the light because their works were evil" (John 3:19).*

At first this seems like a sad and depressing reality, but as far as I can tell, it's true. It was true in Isaiah's day and it is still true in ours. And for us to avoid or to deny its truth is to live in darkness ourselves. We can't do that. We shouldn't do that because at the same time that this is true, that there is darkness in the world, that there are evil people in the world, it is also true that God loves the world.

> *"For God so loved the world that he gave his only son, that whoever believes in him should not perish but have eternal life" (John 3:16).*

That verse goes on to verse 17 and says,

> *"For God did not send his son into the world to condemn the world, but in order that the world might be saved through him."*

So God loves *all* people. That was the original application of this verse back in the first century. It was aimed at the Jewish Temple because the Jews had circled the wagons; they thought it was all about them, that God was only saving faithful Jews. And when Jesus said this, He meant that God loves *everybody*. He doesn't just love the Jews.

But then we also have John 15, written by the same John who wrote John 3:16. This is several chapters later:

> *"If the world hates you, know that it has hated me before it hated you. If you were of the world, the world would love you as its own; but because you are not of the world, but I chose you out of the world, therefore the world hates you" (John 15:18-19).*

Wow! We can also jump to John 3:20, where John says this,

"For everyone who does wicked things hates the light and does not come to the light, lest his works should be exposed."

The presence of God makes people feel guilty. Why would that be in the case? Because we *are* guilty. But at the same time, God's Word, God's way, provides a way to deal with our sin and our guilt. But if we reject God, then we are simply left with our guilt. And people hate that. Everybody hates that. Guilt makes us feel bad. Guilt demands resolution.

"he who sins against me injures himself, all those who hate me love death" (Proverbs 8:36).

We are still talking about Psalm 82. The application or implication is that if you love something, then you hate what threatens the thing that you love. So if you love somebody, then you hate whatever threatens them. If you love your children, you hate the things that threaten your children. And the greater your love is for them, the greater your hatred of those things that threaten them. The more our affection for what is right, the more our disaffection for what is wrong. That's why Psalm 97:10 says, "O you who love the Lord, hate evil!" And Psalm 119:104 says, "Through your precepts I get understanding; therefore I hate every false way."

Love and hate are realities that cannot be denied. The loving and hating are not the issue. The issue is what we love and what we hate, the object of our love and hate. To eliminate hate also eliminates love. Every coin has two sides. Everything we value, every value we have, comes with contrasting perspectives, contrasting affections. Love and hate are not the issue. The issue is what we love and what we hate, the *object* of our affection or disaffection. It is good to love the right things and it is good to hate the wrong things. And it is bad to love the wrong things and it is bad to hate the right things.

All of this, then, sets up Luke 12:49-56. That section tells us about this reality in which we live, that Jesus is talking about. It tells us about Jesus' mission with regard to this reality.

Luke 12:49 reads, "I came to cast fire on the earth." The commentators tell us that this refers not to the hell fire of final judgment, but to the earthly division between believers and unbelievers. Is this true? Is there a stark division between believers and unbelievers? We need to be careful because there are some important issues that we need to lift up, otherwise we are going to get some important things wrong.

Jesus has come to turn unbelievers into believers, to change people, to change humanity. So the distinction between believers and believers is not a hard and fast distinction. In addition, it is not *our* distinction to make. It's *God's* call. Whether you are a believer or not, that's between you and the Lord. The reason I say this is because all believers were once unbelievers. All believers have had a change of heart and mind. So the distinction between believers and unbelievers is fluid because Christ has come to change the hearts and minds of unbelievers and to turn them into believers. There is volatility in that distinction because it can change. We need to be careful and not judge other people harshly because their relationship with Jesus Christ can change.

But if we err, we must always err on the side of grace and mercy, always hoping that God will change hearts and minds. It's never too late for anyone. The thief on the cross has established that. We know that we can't change other people's hearts and minds. We can't even change our own minds, even though our minds change all the time. Are we doing it? Have you ever tried to break a habit? It's harder than it sounds.

But God can change hearts and minds. That's His specialty. So what can we do? We can testify about our own changed hearts and minds. And then God can use that testimony, use our example of that change to help others change. God uses testimonies and examples of faithful Christians throughout history for His purposes, to help other people as they change their minds.

Jesus goes on to say in verse 51,

> *"Do you think that I have come to give peace on earth? No, I tell you, but rather division."*

Truth divides. Truth separates truth from error. It separates; it makes a distinction between what is true and what is false. It identifies what is true and what is not true. But truth also unites people as they then align themselves with truth.

The history of Christianity is the story of the proliferation of denominations, of various divisions. In an attempt to remedy that situation, Christianity, mainline Christianity, over the past hundred years or so has been dominated by the ecumenical movement. The goal of the ecumenical movement has been to unite the various denominations, to overcome our divisions.

After a period of neglect, a result of the Reformation, the word *ecumenical* reappeared in the twentieth century. Various denominations, disturbed by their divisions from one another, which were made particularly apparent by the competitive nature of nineteenth-century missionary activities, began to look for ways to overcome their diverse histories. Following a world-wide conference in Edinburgh in 1910, the word *ecumenism* began to be used. In addition to the concern for unity was the concern for mission. These twin ideas of unity and mission have characterized what has come to be referred to as the ecumenical movement.

The mainline denominations have been caught up in this movement for the last hundred years. St. Paul's is 184 years old, and having been associated with the United Church of Christ for a few decades we understand this because the United Church of Christ was the leading light of the recent ecumenical movement. I also understand it. I grew up in the United Church of Christ. I went to United Church of Christ seminary. I was ordained in the United Church of Christ. And like St. Paul's, I left the United Church of Christ.

Yet, at the same time, we still applaud the early work of the ecumenical movement. Their early work was notable. It was honorable. It was good. We believe in Christian unity and we are saddened by the lack of it.

I mention all of this because Jesus' teaching about this division applies to the ecumenical movement and the desire for the unity of the churches. How so? Well, the United Church of Christ adopted a long time ago the theology of the Unitarian Universalist Association, not officially but functionally. And that theology teaches that

Christ saves all people. It teaches that all people are going to heaven, no matter what. And so the United Church of Christ and the ecumenical movement began to try to define the church to include everybody, the saved and the lost without distinction.

The thinking was that, *if we can just include the values of everybody within the church, then the church will appeal to everybody. Then we'll have unity.* But it hasn't worked out very well, actually. It hasn't worked out because that is not the teaching of the Old Testament nor the teaching of the New Testament. Yet it is true that God desires that all people be saved, 2 Peter 3:9 says,

> *"The Lord is not slow to fulfill his promise as some count slowness, but is patient toward you, not wishing that any should perish, but that all should reach repentance."*

It is true that God wants everybody to be saved. However, many people don't want God's salvation. They don't want anything to do with it. Many people believe it to be a fiction, or a lie, or a bad thing. In addition, the New Testament clearly teaches the reality of hell, and many people reject that. It is a harsh teaching—but true, hell is real.

According to Romans 1 people who refuse the salvation of Jesus Christ get what they want, get what they desire. That's what Romans 1 says. Romans 1 is about the refusal of the gospel. Paul says that God will give them what they want. He will give them over to a reprobate mind. He will let them have what they want. God does that. He lets us have what we want.

> *"Therefore God gave them up in the lusts of their hearts to impurity, to the dishonoring of their bodies among themselves, because they exchanged the truth about God for a lie and worshiped and served the creature rather than the Creator" (Romans 1:24-25).*

And so you've got to *want* the right things, that's the trick. You have to actually *want* it. You have to want the right things. Because if you want the wrong things, God will give them to you. Why would He do that? Because He is not going to force anyone into heaven. He loves us all, but you can't *force* anybody into loving you in return. If you try to do that, that's not love. That is manipulation. And God is not going to do that. God wants willing participation.

And so God dispatches His Holy Spirit to come into our hearts and minds and change what we want, change what we desire, change the way we see the world, to get us into alignment with the way God sees the world. He sees the world truly because He created it. But because God wants our love, He will not force us to love Him in return. We have to come willingly. So it is true that Jesus Christ divides believers from unbelievers because Jesus makes *us* decide. He does not force the outcome of our decision, but He does force us to *choose*.

The larger issue here is that believers and unbelievers are not treated the same by God. We do the same thing in our court systems. We treat law abiding citizens different than those who break the law. The law applies equally to everybody, or it is suppose to. Our American judicial system was designed to treat all people the same by subjecting all people to the same laws. However, if you obey the law, you get one response from the court. But if you break the law, you are treated differently.

There are consequences. There is one law that applies to everybody, but the consequences for law abiders are different from the consequences for law breakers. We do the same thing that God is doing. The same laws apply to everyone equally, but the courts treat violators differently than those who obey the law because behavior has consequences.

The truth is that Jesus Christ both unites and divides people. He unites believers together under the umbrella of God's truth, God's love. In this we see that Christian unity is not something that *we* need to do. That is where the denominations got it wrong. They have been trying to get the denominational constitutions to be in alignment, in agreement. But that hasn't worked, and it is not going to work. It won't work because our constitutions are not eternal in their character. They are temporal. And we can't force temporal creations into eternal reality.

So the way to this unity is to put eternal things together, not to mix temporal things with eternal things. Christ is eternal, and our souls are also eternal. Thus, to be in line with Jesus Christ, we need to be in personal unity with Jesus Christ. Our souls need to be in union with Jesus Christ, matching our eternal souls with His eternal reality. Then, as individuals we are in unity with Christ. And as individuals, the closer we get to Christ, the closer we get to one another.

The focus of Christian unity must be personal unity with Jesus Christ. That is the only unity that will work, because what is eternal in us is then aligned with what is eternal in Christ. This is the unity that Jesus was talking about. And it's not about denominational constitutions. It is a personal reality that we need to realize, to realize it, to make it real. That means that we act as if it's real, because it is.

Unfortunately, the scripture also says that these divisions affect families. And that is an uncomfortable reality in today's world because most families in America today are divided. In fact, American culture encourages and facilitates division. The culture encourages it. This is simply the reality in which we live. And it is not a new reality. It is not a new reality to the world, because it was also true back in the first century. It was true even in the Old Testament. It is a perpetual problem.

And so God through Christ has redefined the family. God's family, the Christian family, is not defined biologically. It is defined Christologically. In the Old Testament the Jews got it wrong. They thought that the truth of God's grace was family oriented. A person needed to be in the Jewish family. One could be born into it, or adopted into it. But they thought that salvation was limited to the Jews. But that was never true. Abraham was to be a blessing for all. Jesus knew this and said, *no, that's not true! God's concern is universal salvation. It applies to everybody.* He said that the Christian family takes precedence over the born-of-the-blood family.

This is a hard lesson to come to terms with. But here is what Jesus said in Matthew 10:37:

> *"Whoever loves father or mother more than me is not worthy of me, and whoever loves son or daughter more than me is not worthy of me."*

This is a difficult teaching because we all have various divisions in our families, whether they are political or religious or whatever. Jesus said that the Christian family actually takes predominance over the born-of-the-blood family. The Christian family is more important than the blood family.

I long for the day when our culture will encourage and facilitate genuine Christian unity, not denominational unity, but real genuine Christian unity, where the people of God unite with Christ. Because real Christian unity is found when Christians are in union with Christ. And this is not something that *we* have to accomplish. It is something we have to realize is already true. It's already the case. We just need to get in line with it. Lord, make it so.

Heavenly Father, we are grateful for the blessings that you have provided for us, for your love and grace and mercy and wisdom. We give you thanks for your presence in our lives, your presence in this church. Help us to be thankful in the midst of all things, not just the good things.

We pray for this church and for her to be a blessing in this community. Help us to be faithful and help the community to see our faithfulness as your blessing.

We also pray for our families and for the divisions that are in our families. We pray that you would overcome our divisions, because only you can do that and only your overcoming will actually overcome them. Help us not to be a hindrance in that regard. Help us not to be a stone of stumbling in the midst of our own families, but to be a facilitator of your grace and your mercy and your wisdom, as best as we are able, relying upon your presence and your power.

We pray against the war that is raging in Ukraine, but actually there are wars going on in lots of different places. We pray for your peace, because in another Scripture you said you bring peace. You bring the peace of Christ, not as the world gives, but as you give,

Father. That's the peace we want. That's the only peace that is real peace.

We also pray for those who are working toward that peace. And we pray against those who are working against that peace, not against them personally, but against their opposition to you. Amen.

August 14, 2022

Healing Disability

9 Then you shall call, and the Lord will answer; you shall cry, and he will say, 'Here I am.' If you take away the yoke from your midst, the pointing of the finger, and speaking wickedness, 10 if you pour yourself out for the hungry and satisfy the desire of the afflicted, then shall your light rise in the darkness and your gloom be as the noonday. 11 And the Lord will guide you continually and satisfy your desire in scorched places and make your bones strong; and you shall be like a watered garden, like a spring of water, whose waters do not fail. 12 And your ancient ruins shall be rebuilt; you shall raise up the foundations of many generations; you shall be called the repairer of the breach, the restorer of streets to dwell in. 13 "If you turn back your foot from the Sabbath, from doing your pleasure on my holy day, and call the Sabbath a delight and the holy day of the Lord honorable; if you honor it, not going your own ways, or seeking your own pleasure, or talking idly; 14 then you shall take delight in the Lord, and I will make you ride on the heights of the earth; I will feed you with the heritage of Jacob your father, for the mouth of the Lord has spoken." —*Isaiah 58:9-14*

10 Now he was teaching in one of the synagogues on the Sabbath. 11 And behold, there was a woman who had had a disabling spirit for eighteen years. She was bent over and could not fully straighten herself. 12 When Jesus saw her, he called her over and said to her, "Woman, you are freed from your disability." 13 And he laid his hands on her, and immediately she was made straight, and she glorified God. 14 But the ruler of the synagogue, indignant because Jesus had healed on the Sabbath, said to the people, "There are six days in which work ought to be done. Come on those days and be healed, and not on the Sabbath day." 15 Then the Lord answered him, "You hypocrites! Does not each of you on the Sabbath untie his ox or his donkey from the manger and lead it away to water it? 16 And ought not this woman, a daughter of Abraham whom Satan bound for eighteen years, be loosed from this bond on the Sabbath day?" 17 As he said these things, all his adversaries were put to shame, and all the people rejoiced at all the glorious things that were done by him.

—Luke 13:10-17

There are several issues in here that we are going to deal with. But I'm afraid that we are so used to hearing arguments about the literal truth of the Bible that it is difficult for us to understand that there can be any other kind of truth other than literal truth. So you need to know that there is a false argument that goes something like this: *If the Bible is not absolutely and literally true, then none of it can be trusted.* You may have heard this argument that says that every word of the Bible has to be absolutely and literally true, or you can't trust anything in the Bible. Well, hogwash! That really isn't true.

For instance Pilate asked Jesus, "What is truth" (John 18:38). Admittedly, truth is a difficult subject. Philosophers, theologians, and scientists have struggled with this concern for millennia. So, it is not likely that such a simple idea as "literal reading of a text" is going to provide much help. Let me share with you some modern history that will help us understand the issue more deeply.

In 1995 the United Nations established a committee to discover the underlying reasons behind the events that occurred in Bosnia and South African apartheid. The committee became known as the *Truth and Reconciliation Committee.*

In their voluminous report in 2000 they provided a new categorization and/or redefinition of "truth." They presented four types of truth. The first one they called "Social truth." When a number of stories of a given society are told publicly, together they form a social truth, or more aptly, a societal truth. We can think of this kind of truth as a social construct. The second kind of truth they called "Personal or Narrative Truth." This is truth is composed of personal recollections and memory. This kind of truth is not the whole of truth, but is composed of integral parts of the truth that lead to "new justice." The third kind of truth they called "Reconciliatory or Healing Truth" (also called "Public Truth"). This kind of truth exposes the "facts" of an event that result in a "healed" or "reconciled" society. The fourth kind of truth they called "Forensic Truth." This is composed of just the bare facts. What happened? To whom? Where? When? How? And who was involved?

Are there really different kinds of truth? Yes, there are. When we ask whether the Bible true, what exactly are we asking? Are we asking if all of the Bible stories actually happened exactly as they are told? Are all of the stories in the Bible literally true? Is this United Nations report *true*? The fact of the matter is not that truth is complicated, but that our understanding of truth is complicated because we are complicated creatures.

In fact, the Bible contains all of these different kinds of truth—and another kind of truth that the United Nations didn't recognize. Let's call this additional kind of truth "spiritual truth." So what is truth? Most of the time that people talk about truth they mean the point or the purpose or the lesson of a story. The truth of a story is the point, the purpose, or the lesson of the facts or the elements involved in the story. Truth is the moral of the story. Truth is not just whatever happened in the story, but it involves our understanding of what happened, and what the story means.

Truth is more than facts. All facts require some sort of context or they don't make any sense. Thus, when we are talking about biblical truth we are talking about God's understanding of what has happened because the Bible is His story. Let's call this "spiritual truth."

In a court of law it is always the facts that are disputed. Each side claims a particular and opposing understanding of the facts of the case. One side argues that this is the way it happened. The opposing side tells a different story, often about the same "facts." They put the facts in a different context. So they are not arguing about the facts. They are arguing about the *interpretation* or *context* of the facts. And court cases get more complicated because some "facts" are allowed by the court and some "facts" are not allowed by the court.

The judge decides which "facts," which interpretation of the "facts," are allowed. And the jury decides which "facts" are actually true, to the best of their ability. So, the truth is that all "facts" require context and interpretation, because it is how the facts are involved in the story, or the case, that provides the truth.

So how do you read the Bible? How are we supposed to read it to understand the truth? First of all, we have to accept the premise of the biblical stories to be faithful and true. We have to believe that the Bible makes sense, that it has been written to convey truth. The determination of whether a particular Bible story is actually and literally true is impossible to determine with any scientific accuracy today. Was the woman literally healed of her flow of blood? Did Jesus actually walk on water? It's impossible today for us to say that these stories are literally true. All we have are the stories. Corroborating evidence is simply not available. We can compare other reports of the story, or of similar stories. But the literal facts of the story are not available to us.

And so we receive the various stories of the Bible in faith. And it is very important that we receive the stories in faith, that we accept the premise of the story. And the premise of the various stories is that they actually happened. The stories that we read are offered as being honest accounts of the facts. The writers are telling us what happened to the best of their ability. If we don't accept the premise of the stories, if we reject the stories as being false or inaccurate, we will miss the point, the purpose, the truth of the stories. In order to understand them we must accept them as true stories.

The story of the healing of the woman with a disabling spirit is presented as a simple fact. We don't know her actual disease, or how it was cured because those "facts" will distract from the moral truth of the story. We must simply accept the story of this woman who had the disabling spirit, that it happened as described. What truth is conveyed by this story? We might ask, what constitutes healing? What does it mean to be healed? What was the result of this healing?

In terms of context, the Greek words *healing* and *salvation* share a common root—*salve*. A salve is an ointment used to heal wounds;

salvation is the healing of a broken relationship with God. Salvation is the healing of our spirit. Whatever meaning the story has will require that we accept its premise, accept the literal reading as being true. And once we accept this as being true, then we can go on and talk about what it means? How is it true? Once we accept the story, we can think about the lesson, moral, or truth it teaches.

The elements of biblical meaning are analogy, symbolism, theology, and application. But another question to ask is: was Jesus' healing miracles for the sake of the individual who was healed? Or for the sake of the larger biblical story? Sure, the healed person benefited, but is that the lesson or moral of the healing story? Let me suggest that it is not. Jesus' healing miracles were given for the sake of the larger story, and as evidence consider the story of the man born blind in John 9. It is a long complicated story, but here is the conclusion:

> *"His disciples asked him, 'Rabbi, who sinned, this man or his parents, that he was born blind?' 'Neither this man nor his parents sinned,' said Jesus, 'but this happened so that the works of God might be displayed in him'" (John 9:2-3).*

His healing wasn't for his own sake. His healing was for the sake of the gospel story. This is important.

When Paul wrote about Israel and baptism he talked about the ancient Israelites passing through the waters as they left Egypt. Paul called that a kind of a baptism.

> *"Now these things took place as examples for us, that we might not desire evil as they did" (1 Corinthians 10:6).*

And what he meant is that those events in the Old Testament took place for the sake of the New Testament writers who would write about them later to reveal the hand of God in history. Applying this idea more generally we see that the healing miracles that Jesus did were not simply for the sake of the individuals who were healed. They were for the sake of the larger story of God's work in the world. Jesus was healing the church, the people of God, not just individuals. He was healing the body of Christ because biblical healings are not simply for the sake of the person who is healed. The fact of the healings established the credibility of the healer.

Yet in the New Testament, the person who did the healing—the apostles also worked healing miracles—was not the healer either. The Person who actually did the healing was God—Father, Son, and Holy Spirit. God did the healing. So the biblical healings are intended to establish the credibility of God in history. Again, Jesus was healing the body of Christ, healing the church, not just healing various individuals.

The larger story demonstrates that the healing of individuals contributed to the healing of the church. Why? Because those who needed healing, this woman and others who needed healing, were not allowed into the Temple because they were not whole. They were flawed. The rules of the Temple forbade them entry. They were barred from participating with the people of God. Those who needed healing were not allowed into the Temple, not allowed in the church, the body of Christ, the people of God.

And the result of Jesus healing was that those who were healed praised God and went into the temple. Or they showed themselves to the priests so that they would be allowed into the Temple. But when they did this, people freaked out. The establishment was not pleased.

The Temple establishment didn't think that it needed to be healed. So when Jesus healed this woman a Temple leader accused Him of breaking the Sabbath. He accused Jesus of violating the law. So Jesus called him a hypocrite because he misunderstood the whole meaning and the purpose of God's law. Note that it was a *leader* of the synagogue who misunderstood the law.

Did Jesus actually violate the law? Well, he actually did violate the ruler's *understanding* of the law. But Jesus argued that the ruler's understanding of the law was not God's understanding of the law. And the truth of the law is God's understanding, not his, not ours. God defines His law. We are not to redefine it to suit our own desires or our own understanding.

In the larger sense of God's story the events of this particular story take place in a kind of court of public opinion. A guy comes into the temple and there is this conversation that happens. It's as if the court of public opinion is the highest court in the land. This idea still rings true today.

In our world today, we have governmental agencies who violate the law that they established. Various government agencies and officers of the law fail to enforce various laws. Why? Well, because they believe those laws to be flawed. So they are prosecuting their case in the court of public opinion in order to change the law. It's weird, but that seems to be what is happening.

> *"As he said these things, all his adversaries were put to shame, and all the people rejoiced at all the glorious things that were done by him" (Luke 13:17).*

Jesus made His case that healing belongs to God and that the ruler didn't understand the law. And the people applauded! Jesus defeated the ruler in the court of public opinion, and all of the people rejoiced at the glorious things that were done by Him.

The people, public opinion, sided with Jesus. And with that the story established the credibility of the Healer, the credibility of God, of Jesus. So the healing story of the woman with a disabling spirit is not really about the woman at all. It's about the disabling spirit that kept her from being upright, that kept her apart from the people of God, that kept her outside of the Temple community.

It's a story about Jesus doing God's will to heal the church, to heal the synagogue, to heal the body of Christ. It's a story about brokenhearted people who need the wholeness and holiness of God, but they are kept out of fellowship by the rules of the established churches. It's a story about getting into right relationship with God and reentering into fellowship and communion with the people of God. That's what the story is about.

The healing story of the woman with a disabling spirit is not about the woman. It's about God and about God's church, God's people. It's about the brokenness of the church, the brokenness of the Temple, the brokenness of the people of God. And how they are healed by the spirit of Christ, and their reestablishment among the people of God. Christ healed her in order that she could be reunited or come back into the people of God. That's the story.

Let's go back to the Isaiah reading because the lectionary links these readings. Isaiah was actually a priest, not a prophet. He had a job in the Temple. Most of the other prophets were farmers, outsiders, who came into Jerusalem and complained. But Isaiah lived in the city. But like the prophets, Isaiah called God's people to repentance. He called the people of God to repent.

But when God first called Isaiah into ministry God said, *I want you to go call these people and tell them to repent, but they are not going to listen to you, they are not going to hear you. But don't worry about that.* God told Isaiah to tell them about the destruction that will come upon them because they will not repent. God said that a final judgment would come upon them by the hand of the Babylonians, some hundred and twenty years after Isaiah. Among Isaiah's numerous indictments of the leadership and the people of Judah, God provided a promise of restoration, a promise of judgment, *yes*, a promise of punishment, *yes!*

But God would not allow Israel to be completely destroyed, which was the fate of so many of the other nations that had fallen to the fate of Assyria at the time. Assyria was the military might of the day, and it conquered many nations. Listen to this scripture again.

> *"Then you shall call, and the Lord will answer; you shall cry, and he*
> *will say, 'Here I am.' If you take away the yoke from your midst, the*
> *pointing of the finger, and speaking wickedness, 10 if you pour your-*
> *self out for the hungry and satisfy the desire of the afflicted, then shall*
> *your light rise in the darkness and your gloom be as the noonday. 11*
> *And the Lord will guide you continually and satisfy your desire in*
> *scorched places and make your bones strong; and you shall be like a*
> *watered garden, like a spring of water, whose waters do not fail. 12*
> *And your ancient ruins shall be rebuilt; you shall raise up the founda-*
> *tions of many generations; you shall be called the repairer of the*
> *breach, the restorer of streets to dwell in. 13 "If you turn back your*
> *foot from the Sabbath, from doing your pleasure on my holy day, and*
> *call the Sabbath a delight and the holy day of the Lord honorable; if*
> *you honor it, not going your own ways, or seeking your own pleasure,*

or talking idly; 14 then you shall take delight in the Lord, and I will make you ride on the heights of the earth; I will feed you with the heritage of Jacob your father, for the mouth of the Lord has spoken" (Isaiah 58:9–14).

God promised renewal of the Temple. This was written a thousand years before Jesus. And it was still a problem in Jesus' time. It's still a problem today! What is the message that people are so unwilling to hear?

God is saying, *if you continue in your own ways, here are the consequences, and they are not going to be pretty. But if you will take up my yoke, do good things, be the people I'm calling you to be,* says Jesus, *then all of these blessings shall be yours.*

It is a double-sided promise that if you're disobedient to God, bad things are going to happen. If you are obedient, the blessings of God will come to you. Does this promise still hold today? It does!

Let us pray. God, our fears and prejudices run deep. Sometimes we can only see our own point of view. We stick with those who are like us, rarely venturing outside our comfort zones. We do not hear those crying for justice and true peace. We blame those who are suffering and in need instead of standing by them. We deny the power of your gospel to unite us with those who are different from us. Lord, give us eyes to see and ears to hear. Open us to the new possibilities of life for all of your people and use us to enact new life that is given in Christ.

We are so grateful for your love and grace and mercy and wisdom. Grateful that you have inserted yourself into our lives personally, and into our life in this church. We give you thanks. We give you praise. Even in the midst of so many bad things and such darkness that we see in our world, we give you thanks and praise because we know that you are good all the time and that your ways are good, and that you are calling us to goodness and to health and wholeness.

And yet, we struggle because it seems like the darkness is growing. It seems to us that things are worse than they used to be. So help us to praise you, Lord! Because the only reason that we are able to see the wickedness of the world is because you have shown us your goodness, and in comparison to that, we now see how bad our wickedness, human wickedness, is. As you reveal yourself more and more, we see more and more our own failures and foibles and follies. And so the darkness that we see is really a result of you revealing yourself in our midst, showing us what true light, what real goodness looks like.

And then we look at our world and weep. So be with us, Father, and help us to focus on the light, not on the darkness. Help us to share the good things. Help us to praise you in everything. Help us to be eucharistic people. Help us to be thankful, even in the midst of difficulties and troubles, even in the midst of pain and loss. Help us to be thankful because you are with us and you are reshaping this world into Jesus' likeness. Amen.

August 21, 2022

Kindness

Let brotherly love continue. 2 Do not neglect to show hospitality to
strangers, for thereby some have entertained angels unawares. 3 Remember those who are in prison, as though in prison with them, and
those who are mistreated, since you also are in the body. 4 Let marriage be held in honor among all, and let the marriage bed be unde-
filed, for God will judge the sexually immoral and adulterous. 5
Keep your life free from love of money, and be content with what
you have, for he has said, "I will never leave you nor forsake you." 6
So we can confidently say, "The Lord is my helper; I will not fear;
what can man do to me?" 7 Remember your leaders, those who
spoke to you the word of God. Consider the outcome of their way of
life, and imitate their faith. 8 Jesus Christ is the same yesterday and
today and forever. —Hebrews 13:1-8, 15-16

1 One Sabbath, when Jesus went to eat in the house of a prominent
Pharisee, he was being carefully watched. 7 When he noticed how the
guests picked the places of honor at the table, he told them this parable: 8 "When someone invites you to a wedding feast, do not take the
place of honor, for a person more distinguished than you may have
been invited. 9 If so, the host who invited both of you will come and
say to you, 'Give this person your seat.' Then, humiliated, you will
have to take the least important place. 10 But when you are invited,
take the lowest place, so that when your host comes, he will say to
you, 'Friend, move up to a better place.' Then you will be honored in
the presence of all the other guests. 11 For all those who exalt themselves will be humbled, and those who humble themselves will be exalted." 12 Then Jesus said to his host, "When you give a luncheon or

dinner, do not invite your friends, your brothers or sisters, your relatives, or your rich neighbors; if you do, they may invite you back and so you will be repaid. 13 But when you give a banquet, invite the poor, the crippled, the lame, the blind, 14 and you will be blessed. Although they cannot repay you, you will be repaid at the resurrection of the righteous." —*Luke 14:1, 7-14*

I'm going to explain this Scripture today in a way that you probably haven't heard before. But it's not a new teaching. It's a very old teaching that has been neglected and forgotten. It's not simply for you who are here this morning. It's also for others beyond these walls. It's for community renewal. I pray that people will find it interesting enough to take it seriously, and maybe even share with someone. It is a message that is desperately needed in our world today. Lord, give people ears to hear.

We need to begin by setting the context of this story, and the context comes from the book of Genesis.

"And God made the beasts of the earth according to their kinds and the livestock according to their kinds, and everything that creeps on the ground according to its kind. And God saw that it was good" (Genesis 1:25).

We begin by talking about kindness, and we begin with the definition of *kind*. Why begin with the word *kind*? Because God used that particular word. The dictionary tells us that a *kind* is a group or class usually distinguished by fundamental or essential characteristics. Dogs are a kind, horses are a kind, cows are a kind, and humans are a kind. There are a lot of different sorts of dogs, but they are all dogs. They are all of the same kind. Horses are a kind. There are a lot of different kinds of horses, but all horses are of the same kind.

In addition, human beings are a kind. And there are a lot of different sorts of human beings, but all human beings are of one kind. Another word that we don't use much anymore is *kin*. You may have heard the phrase, *Kith and kin*? *Kith* is probably a version of *kiss*, and it refers to our relatives, whom we kiss. And *kin* is a shortened version of *kind*. Your *kin* is your *kind*, your relatives.

When God created a new humanity in Christ Jesus, He created a new *kind* of human being, a new family group, or family tree, a genus. But it is not a genetic tree, but a spiritual tree. Our lineage in Christ is spiritual not genetic, behavioral not biological. It's about grace, not race; about bread, not blood.

"Brotherly love" (Hebrews 13:1) is about this new Jesus kind of human being, about the family of Christ, about our common ancestry in Christ, and the fundamental or essential characteristics that unite us, that put us into the same group, the same *kind*. There is a fundamental or essential characteristic, or family of characteristics, that unites all Christians, that put us into the same group, that put us into the same family, that put us into the same kind, or the same *kin*.

This is why Paul told the Hebrews to remember those in prison as if they are in prison with them. (They were in prison because of their faith, not for common crimes.) Christians are to remember all who are in Christ and who are mistreated because they are all part of the same body, the body of Christ. The body of Christ is the new kind of human being. And as a body it is both singular and plural. It is one, but is made up of many parts. Elsewhere Paul said, *if your little toe hurts, your whole body knows about it* (1 Corinthians 12:12-27).

What holds this body together is Christ. What allows it to function as a body is the Holy Spirit. The one body of Christ, the church, has many parts. It has one purpose, and many functions. It has one goal, and many strategies, one common center, but many diverse circumferences. The body is both singular and plural at the same time, but in different ways.

Another definition of the word *body* defines it as a group. We are a body. This church is a body, and when we gather as a body for a congregational meeting, we ask the body to vote. Many members vote on behalf of the whole group, the body. It's the same word in English. But in Greek Paul uses two different words that are both translated as *body*: σάρξ and σῶμα.[4]

---

4 Paul plays with these words in ways that are not captured in the English. See *Arsy Varsy—Reclaiming The Gospel in First Corinthians*, Phillip A. Ross, Pilgrim Platform, Marietta, Ohio, 2008.

Biologically, the thing that makes a *kind* is the ability to reproduce the same *kind*. That is part of the biological definition of *kind*. Dogs cannot breed with cats, nor horses with cows. People cannot breed with monkeys because they are different kinds. And this is why Paul immediately went to a discussion of the marriage bed (Hebrews 13:4). Individuals who can reproduce compose a *kind*. Human beings can reproduce human beings, so humanity is a *kind*. However, just because people can reproduce doesn't mean that they should.

In order to produce kindness based on love, or loving kindness, love must precede, protect, and reproduce love. So God invented marriage as the engine of loving kindness. We might also call it a *loving kindred*. Marriage is the engine, the way, the means that God uses to produce loving kindness, loving kin. However, loving kindness is not a being, it is a social construction. So it gets produced socially. Love requires others, so love is necessarily social. Christlike love is how Christians are supposed to relate to one another.

The word *marriage* has fallen on hard times. So I like to call it *holy matrimony*. Originally God created marriage or holy matrimony to be a three-way relationship, not a two-way relationship. It was a relationship between a man and God and a woman. If you take God out of it, it isn't what God created. So by calling it *holy matrimony* we emphasize God's involvement. God is not just creating new human beings, He is creating a new *kind* of human being, a kind of human love, a loving kindness that issues out of God's love.

The purpose of human marriage is not just to produce children, nor to simply provide companionship. Rather, the purpose of human marriage in Christ (holy matrimony) is to produce loving kindness, loving kin. Thus, in Christ we are no longer *homo sapiens, but we become homo Christos.*[5] We are Christ creatures, and as Christ creatures we are to exemplify loving kindness in our marriages and in our selves and in our churches. Loving kindness is the essential characteristic that is to define and identify us as *homo Christos* (Christians).

5 *Sapien* is from *sapience,* which means wisdom. H*omo sapien* means wisdom fused to flesh, *homo Christos* means Christ fused to flesh.

Paul then warns Christians about sexual immorality and adultery because of the intimate relationship between marriage, sex, and loving kindness. Notice how many of the problems in the world today are related to getting sex wrong, ignoring of denying the various biblical instructions about sex, ignoring what the Bible calls sexual morality. Think about sex and its relationship to the fruits of the spirit.

> *"But But the fruit of the Spirit is love, joy, peace, patience, kindness, goodness, faithfulness, gentleness, self-control; against such things there is no law" (Galatians 5:22-23).*

Each of these fruits of the spirit have a roll to play in sex, and the place to practice them first and foremost is in the marriage relationship. When we get them right in marriage, life goes well. And when we don't, life doesn't go so well. I'm talking about sex and marriage because Paul brought it up.

> *"Let marriage be held in honor among all, and let the marriage bed be undefiled, for God will judge the sexually immoral and adulterous" (Hebrews 13:4).*

Paul was saying, *don't get love wrong*: "Keep your life free from love of money" (Hebrews 13:5). This is huge! In order to understand why Paul went from marriage to money we need to see what they have in common. Both marriage and money are means of reproduction, and both are built on promise-keeping. Reproduction in marriage occurs through sex. Reproduction in money occurs through compound interest, which gave rise to capitalism, which gave rise to the modern world. Compound interest is a kind of usury, which is forbidden in Scripture, Old Testament and New.

In today's world, money is reproduced or created through investment. The process is complex, but in short, our money supply can grow through proper investment. It reproduces itself. But proper investment takes time and attention if it is not to fall into greed and various forms of corruption.

"For the love of money is a root of all kinds of evils. It is through this craving that some have wandered away from the faith and pierced themselves with many pangs" (1 Timothy 6:10).

Love is defined as time and attention. We love what we give our time and attention to. And this brings us full circle. Paul says, *give your time and attention to your marriage, and not to money*. We only have so much time and attention, so what we give to the one we must take from the other. This is a very literal reading of Paul's instructions here. He is not saying that we should give *no* time and attention to money, only that we need to keep our priorities straight: marriage is more important than money. He concludes this section by saying that this will always be true in human history: "Jesus Christ is the same yesterday and today and forever" (Hebrews 13:8).

The Luke 14 Scripture then addresses the primary human characteristic that messes our godly priorities up: self-importance. When we think we are important, we put ourselves ahead of others. And the thing that makes most people feel important is money. The more money we have, the more important we feel. And other people confirm this because most people believe it. Money is a measure of value, and the more money we have, the more valuable we think we are—and other people think the same thing. And by thinking it, they/we make it so.

"Power tends to corrupt, and absolute power corrupts absolutely," said Lord Acton. Here's the deal: money is power. And money tends to corrupt because it steals time and attention from our marriages. We only have so much time and attention, and to give it to the one takes it from the other. Thus, the new human kind created by Jesus Christ is not, and must not be based on money. It is to be based on marriage (love), not genetic inheritance or biological relationships. Rather, our spiritual inheritance is the root or engine of holy matrimony—the threesome of man/God/woman.

We are to be kind to one another because we are of the same *kind*; we are family. But our family is the body of Christ, and all who manifest the fruits of the Spirit are in Christ's family, Christ's body on earth. The Bible speaks of Jesus Christ as the bridegroom and the church as the bride of Christ.

> *"Let us rejoice and exult and give him the glory, for the marriage of the Lamb has come, and his Bride has made herself ready; it was granted her to clothe herself with fine linen, bright and pure"— for the fine linen is the righteous deeds of the saints" (Revelation 19:7-8).*

> *"And I saw the holy city, new Jerusalem, coming down out of heaven from God, prepared as a bride adorned for her husband" (Revelation 21:2).*

Christ's church is to be based upon marriage, but it's not the blood aspects of marriage. Christ's church is based upon the legal aspects of marriage. Marriage is a legal thing. But in terms of Christianity, the marriage of the church to Jesus Christ is not a genetic or a biological relationship. That is the key here. It is not of the flesh. Rather the key is our spiritual inheritance. This is the root of Christianity and the root or the engine of holy matrimony, that threesome between man and God and woman.

And so we are to be kind to one another because we are of the same *kind*. Christians are family to one another. Unfortunately, not every person alive is in this new family yet. Only those who actually practice the fruits of the Spirit. Anyone can become a member, not simply by joining a church, but by actually practicing the fruits of the Spirit. Of course, if you do practice them, you will want to be with others who practice them, and that involves the church. This is the Church Universal, the body of Christ on earth. This is what God is doing in Jesus Christ. This is why we are called into the church.

Heavenly Father, we are so grateful for Jesus Christ, grateful that you sent Jesus on this mission in this world, to create this new family, this body of Christ. We are grateful that you have inserted yourself into our lives in whatever ways. We thank you for this church and for her ministry.

Of course, we have our better days and our worst days. Often, we are like Peter, we take two steps forward and one step back. And churches are the same way. And over our long history, we have taken steps forward and steps backward, and yet we are still here, Lord, still proclaiming your love, your grace, your mercy, your wisdom in the midst of this community.

Knowing that you are always the same, we give you thanks and praise for that. And we pray that you would be with us. Help us to be who you have called us to be. Give us the vision to see it and the intelligence to understand it, and the courage to walk it out in our lives, in the midst of a world gone mad. Help us to be the people that you have called us to be. Help us define ourselves not as who we are in ourselves, not by our past, but by who we are in you, who we are as finished products in the kingdom of heaven. That is where we are headed. That's who we are. Help us to real-ize that.

We know that we don't always do a very good job of manifesting it. We know that, and we confess that, and we lean into your Holy Spirit to help us be better day by day. And we pray for this world. We pray for those who don't know you. We pray for those who hate you. We pray for those who ignore you. We pray that you would pour out your Holy Spirit in such a way that it would be attractive and would cause people to hear it, and see it, and conform their lives to it.

Again, we pray for those who are for you and against those who are against you, not against them personally, but against their lack of understanding of who you are and what you're doing. We pray for our community. We pray that you would pour out your Holy Spirit and touch people's hearts and lives and draw them into you, Father. We pray, not only for our own little church, but we pray for a renewal of our community. We also pray for a renewal of the world because that is your mission, Father. But we know that we are weak reads, that there is not much we can do about the world. But we can live our own lives to the glory of God. And as it turns out, that is really all you ask. So help us to do that, Father.

August 21, 2022

Prepare Ye!

4 I thank my God always when I remember you in my prayers, 5
because I hear of your love and of the faith that you have toward the
Lord Jesus and for all the saints, 6 and I pray that the sharing of
your faith may become effective for the full knowledge of every good
thing that is in us for the sake of Christ. 7 For I have derived much
joy and comfort from your love, my brother, because the hearts of the
saints have been refreshed through you. 8 Accordingly, though I am
bold enough in Christ to command you to do what is required, 9 yet
for love's sake I prefer to appeal to you—I, Paul, an old man and
now a prisoner also for Christ Jesus—10 I appeal to you for my
child, Onesimus, whose father I became in my imprisonment. 11
(Formerly he was useless to you, but now he is indeed useful to you
and to me.) 12 I am sending him back to you, sending my very heart.
13 I would have been glad to keep him with me, in order that he
might serve me on your behalf during my imprisonment for the
gospel, 14 but I preferred to do nothing without your consent in order
that your goodness might not be by compulsion but of your own ac-
cord. 15 For this perhaps is why he was parted from you for a while,
that you might have him back forever, 16 no longer as a bondservant
but more than a bondservant, as a beloved brother—especially to me,
but how much more to you, both in the flesh and in the Lord.

—Philemon 1:4-16

25 Now great crowds accompanied him, and he turned and said to
them, 26 "If anyone comes to me and does not hate his own father
and mother and wife and children and brothers and sisters, yes, and
even his own life, he cannot be my disciple. 27 Whoever does not

bear his own cross and come after me cannot be my disciple. 28 For which of you, desiring to build a tower, does not first sit down and count the cost, whether he has enough to complete it? 29 Otherwise, when he has laid a foundation and is not able to finish, all who see it begin to mock him, 30 saying, 'This man began to build and was not able to finish.' 31 Or what king, going out to encounter another king in war, will not sit down first and deliberate whether he is able with ten thousand to meet him who comes against him with twenty thousand? 32 And if not, while the other is yet a great way off, he sends a delegation and asks for terms of peace. 33 So therefore, any one of you who does not renounce all that he has cannot be my disciple.

—Luke 14:25-33

This is another hard section of Scripture. And I have to tell you, I wouldn't have chosen this, but it was given to me by the Lectionary. It's in the Book, so I've got to deal with it, right? I beg your indulgence, and I pray that you will hear the Word of the Lord. So just open your ears and listen for the Lord. We begin with the first Scripture from Philemon.

Philemon owned slaves. And Onesimus was a runaway slave who had been saved by Jesus Christ, and had found his way to Paul. Philemon, his master, had been cruel, but after Onesimus had run away, the Master was also saved. This is the situation of the story. Paul then sent Onesimus back to his former master, Philemon, with a letter asking the master to treat Onesimus as a brother in Christ. And that drops us right into the issue of slavery.

Slavery has been a reality in every era of human history. Generally it was the result of war, where the victors enslaved the vanquished. That's just the way things were done. Slavery has been an eternal blight on human history, and more recently, a blight on American history. However, we must remember that the movement to end slavery began in the Christian West, in Britain in the 1700s.

That movement was also very active in America during the same period, and ever since. The movement to end slavery was engendered by the Bible, and the vast majority of those opposed to slavery were Evangelical Christians. Yet, in spite of all of this, some Christians in the American South defended slavery prior to and during the Civil War. At the time the economy of the South, and much of the country, was dependent on slavery—both North and South. Cotton was the primary product of the South, and was funded by banks in the North. All of that is true! We cannot and must not deny it.

Several Southern Christian theologians noted accurately that the Bible tolerated slavery, even citing this letter of Philemon, where Paul sent a runaway slave back to his master to continue in the master-slave relationship. Paul sent this letter to Philemon with Onesimus. Think about the dynamics of this: Both Philemon and Onesimus had been saved. So, Paul sent Onesimus back to Philemon, back to his slavery with this letter. Note also that the Bible regularly refers the apostles as slaves or bond-servants to Christ (2 Timothy 2:24, 1 Peter 2:16, Colossians 1:7, 2 Peter 1:1, Jude 1:1, Revelation 1:1, 7:3).

Now jump back into the late 1700s and think about our own Marietta history, because Marietta has a very interesting history. Founded in 1789 by an act of Congress, Marietta was settled by Revolutionary war generals because Congress gave them land rather than money as payment for their military service. Prior to the founding of the United States of America in 1776 there were no national funds.

The people who were involved in the founding of Marietta also played an instrumental role in the founding of this nation. Originally Marietta was the launching platform into the Northwest territory, which seems weird today, because Marietta is so far from the Northwest. But at the time, Marietta was considered to be part of the Northwest because it was a launching place of Northwest discovery. So the founding of the Northwest territory began here in Marietta. Why is that important? Because it was the people in Marietta who insisted that slavery be kept out of the Northwest territories.

It is important that we not deny any of this: America's involvement in slavery or America's campaign to end slavery. Nor can we deny Christianity's involvement in slavery, nor Christianity's campaign to end slavery. All of these forces are still in play today.

Coming back to the Scripture, we need to consider the faith of Onesimus, the runaway slave who had been saved by Jesus Christ, and who willingly returned to his master. This faithful slave who had been freed in Christ agreed to return to slavery as an act of faithfulness to the Lord, in order to witness the love of Jesus Christ to his master. That is faithfulness!

People sometimes think that we in the modern world have ended slavery. The North won the Civil War, and Lincoln emancipated the slaves by passing a law in 1863. But Lincoln didn't actually free all of the approximately four million men, women, and children held in slavery in the United States when he signed the formal Emancipation Proclamation. The document applied only to enslaved people in the Confederacy, and not to those in the border states that remained loyal to the Union. And the Civil War did not end until 1865. Nonetheless, that Proclamation marked a crucial shift in in Lincoln's views and the views of the American people regarding slavery. The fight against slavery was not over, it was just beginning.

So, now it's 2022. Have we eliminated slavery yet? We have certainly put a huge dent in it. The worst elements of slavery have been eliminated in Western civilization, for the most part. People don't own people anymore. And much of the worst cruelty has been abandoned by civilized people. But as we know from the history of our own lifetimes, the fight to end slavery is not over.

To better understand the issues we need to better understand slavery. What is it exactly? Here's how the Bible defines slavery:

> *"The rich rules over the poor, and the borrower is the slave of the lender" (Proverbs 22:7).*

If slavery is essentially a financial relationship, as taught by the Bible, then there is more slavery today than every before in history. Modern economics functions on the basis of credit, on borrowing, which means that people in debt are slaves to the lending institutions. If this is true, modern slavery is much different from ancient slavery, for the most part.

Human trafficking is also a kind of slavery, as is illegal immigration where people agree to work off a debt paid to coyotes who provide transportation into America or Europe. This used to be called "indentured slavery," and many, people of every color and ethnicity have a history of involvement in indentured slavery. It took money to settle the new continent, and before Western people got here and established colonies, there was no money here. It was provided from Europeans, who saw the development of America as an investment. They put money up front with the expectation to be paid back with interest as colonies developed. In this sense American was founded by a slave or debt based economy.

Slavery has not been abolished in America. But as far as I know people are not clamoring to emigrate into China, Russia, or India. And today paying off the cost of illegal immigration often gets people involved in the illegal drug business or illicit sex work, both of which perpetuate slavery.

Paul referred to Onesimus as a "bondservant," a person who was working off a debt, a bond. So Paul asked Onesimus to finish working off his debt to Philemon, and he asked Philemon to treat Onesimus well, even as a brother in Christ. But he did not ask Philemon to forgive the debt and free Onesimus from his prior obligation. And that meant that Onesimus would willingly continue in his bondservant role. This is important because a bondservant is a person in debt.

The purpose of the Emancipation Proclamation was to end perpetual slavery, but it couldn't be done all at once. It began a process that is still underway. The purpose was to end human ownership of other human beings.

Today in America people are not owned by other people. But are people in perpetual debt? The bank does not own the homeowner, but neither does the homeowner own the home. For the most part, banks own the property, and the homeowner is a bondservant to the bank. At least it seems this way to me.

"If anyone comes to me and does not hate his own father and mother and wife and children and brothers and sisters, yes, and even his own life, he cannot be my disciple" (Luke 14:26).

The Greek word translated "hate" is a Semitic expression for loving less. It is related to the English prefix "miso," as in misanthrope (a hater of humanity) and misogyny (hatred of women). The best way to understand this is in the context of the Shema:

"Hear, O Israel! The Lord is our God, the Lord is one! You shall love the Lord your God with all your heart and with all your soul and with all your might" (Deuteronomy 6:4-5).

The Lord is one. How can we understand this? Let's go back to school for a minute. We need to go back to math class because we're talking about numbers. Mathematically, there are two kinds of numbers. Cardinal numbers, also known as counting numbers, are used to specify quantities. They identify how many; 1, 2, 3, 4, 5, etc. Ordinal numbers indicate rank, order, or position. They identify order: first, second, third, etc. You may not have thought about this before, but this applies to God. God is not simply one in terms of quantity or cardinality. God is also first in terms of order or ordinality. God's cardinality has to do with the unity of the Godhead. And God's ordinality has to do with God's rank of importance in the life of humanity.

Moses and Jesus were saying that God must be the peoples' first priority, before father, mother, wife, husband, children, brother, sister. Or switch it around, we must love God more than we love our families. The idea of hatred here means that we must love our families less than we love God. The primary duty of a disciple is to always consider God first. So, when we plan something, we need to "consider the cost." Not simply the cost of the project, but the cost of putting God first.

"So therefore, any one of you who does not renounce all that he has cannot be my disciple" (Luke 14:33).

This simply means that disciples of Jesus must prioritize God above their possessions, as well as their families. God is more important than all of our worldly goods. God is more important than our families. This is fairly easy to say, although it makes us uncomfortable, but it is difficult to live out. God is not interested in us making a pledge to put Him first. He knows that we treat our vows lightly, that we don't always follow through on our commitments. God wants us to live our promises out, to put them into practice.

It doesn't hurt anything to make promises, as long as we keep our word. The failure to keep our promises destroys the social fabric of a community and the integrity of the individual. Let's not do that. Let's keep our promises beginning with our first promise to love God above all else.

Heavenly Father, this is a hard word that you've given us. Help us to understand that, in spite of the fact of its difficulty, it is true. And in spite of the fact that we cannot live it out in our own strength, you have dispatched your Holy Spirit to strengthen us, to provide for us what we need, what we can't provide for ourselves. The strength that we don't have comes from your Holy Spirit.

So help us to open our hearts and minds, and to depend on your Holy Spirit. Open our hearts and minds as we pray to you, Lord, may your Holy Spirit to lead us and guide us. But help us also to know that the way that You lead us and guide us is through your Word. And yes, your Word does come to us in our thoughts, but the most reliable place we find your Word is in the Bible. So if we want to know what you want us to do, we need to read the Bible. We need to be familiar with Scripture.

So give us that commitment, Father, and make it not just a promise to do it, but help us to actually do it, to open your Book day by day, because it's a big Book. And then dispatch your Holy Spirit to help us understand it.

Father, we are, again, grateful for your presence in our lives, grateful for your presence in this church, grateful for your presence in this world. We are grateful for your demand that we end slavery, slavery of one another. And the way you ask us to end slavery is that you ask us to be willing slaves to Jesus Christ, to do His bidding in our lives, to be of service to our brothers and sisters, to be of service to our society.

Even when Israel was held in captivity in Babylon, the Lord instructed them to be fruitful, to be helpful to the society that had captured them and enslaved them, to be a blessing to that society. So help us, Father, to live out of that model in our lives.

Help us to be who you have called us to be. Give us willing hearts, willing minds. Help us to understand what you have called us to do and to be. And then give us opportunities and courage to live it out, in Jesus name. Amen.

August 27, 2022

Formerly

*12 I thank him who has given me strength, Christ Jesus our Lord,
because he judged me faithful, appointing me to his service, 13 though
formerly I was a blasphemer, persecutor, and insolent opponent. But I
received mercy because I had acted ignorantly in unbelief, 14 and the
grace of our Lord overflowed for me with the faith and love that are
in Christ Jesus. 15 The saying is trustworthy and deserving of full
acceptance, that Christ Jesus came into the world to save sinners, of
whom I am the foremost. 16 But I received mercy for this reason, that
in me, as the foremost, Jesus Christ might display his perfect patience
as an example to those who were to believe in him for eternal life. 17
To the King of the ages, immortal, invisible, the only God, be honor
and glory forever and ever. Amen. —1 Timothy 1:12-17*

*Now the tax collectors and sinners were all drawing near to hear him.
2 And the Pharisees and the scribes grumbled, saying, "This man receives sinners and eats with them." 3 So he told them this parable: 4
"What man of you, having a hundred sheep, if he has lost one of
them, does not leave the ninety-nine in the open country, and go after
the one that is lost, until he finds it? 5 And when he has found it, he
lays it on his shoulders, rejoicing. 6 And when he comes home, he
calls together his friends and his neighbors, saying to them, 'Rejoice
with me, for I have found my sheep that was lost.' 7 Just so, I tell
you, there will be more joy in heaven over one sinner who repents
than over ninety-nine righteous persons who need no repentance. 8
"Or what woman, having ten silver coins, if she loses one coin, does
not light a lamp and sweep the house and seek diligently until she
finds it? 9 And when she has found it, she calls together her friends*

and neighbors, saying, 'Rejoice with me, for I have found the coin that I had lost.' 10 Just so, I tell you, there is joy before the angels of God over one sinner who repents." —*Luke 15:1-10*

The faith that Paul had was not his own. It was given to him as a gift. Faith in Christ is not the result of anything that *we* do. It is the result of what *Christ* has done for us. This is the heart of the gospel, the good news of Jesus Christ. God has created a new human *kind* in Jesus Christ. He has already acted on our behalf. He has taken the first step. And what has he done? In Christ God has already created a new human kind.

In Christ we are no longer *homo sapien*, we are *homo Christos. Homo sapien*, from the word *sapience*, is wisdom fused to humanity. The Old Testament has proven that human wisdom is not enough. *Homo Christos* is Christ fused to humanity.

God didn't ask us if we want to be a new kind of person. He sent His Son to make it happen. It is a reality, a done deal. We can deny it, but we can't stop it. We can ignore it, but it won't ignore us. It is the truth, and the truth does not depend on us to make it true. Truth is true regardless of what we think about it.

Paul wrote to Timothy (v. 12) that Christ had judged him faithful, and appointed him to service. Christ did not ask Paul if he wanted to get with the program. Previously, prior to Paul's conversion, he had been a blasphemer, a persecutor, and an insolent opponent of Jesus Christ (v. 13). Jesus did not ask Paul to receive Him in his heart. He didn't ask Paul anything. Well, He actually did. He asked, "Saul, Saul, why are you persecuting me?" (Acts 9:4). But that's not the kind of question that wants an answer. It is more of an accusation than a question.

Christ then told Paul: "enter the city, and you will be told what you are to do" (v. 6). Paul was not asked what he would like to do, he was told what he would do. Paul was not given any choices. We like to think of Christianity as a choice that people can make if they are so inclined. But that is not the story of the gospel! Jesus never gave anyone a choice. That might sound surprising to you, but I want you to think about it. Read your Bible carefully and listen carefully.

Jesus never asked, *Would you like to be my disciple?* No! Jesus gave people a command: *Follow Me! Take up your cross!* He didn't say, *Would you like to take up your cross?* No one likes the idea of suffering or losing their life, not even for a good cause.

Over the eons the gospel message of Jesus Christ has been domesticated, neutered, defanged, or declawed. In today's world the gospel has no bite, no sting. It asks people, *pretty please?* It begs for your attention, and it garners little to no attention, and most often falls flat. It is easy to ignore the gospel in our day because it makes no demand. *Would you like to come to church with me?*

Christianity was a growing movement in Paul's day. And Paul had been charged by the Temple establishment to get rid of those who followed Christ. They commissioned Paul as a kind of policeman who went out to find Christians and change their minds or eliminate them. That was his job. He had a team and Temple resources to help him do that job. Remember at that time Paul was a Pharisee when Jesus called him on the road to Damascus (Acts 9).

Later, Paul wrote to Timothy that he had received mercy, but how did Paul receive mercy? For Paul the mercy was not an abstract idea about God's kindness, but was very real, physically real. The light of Christ had blinded him, and he was led into a Christian community to receive healing and recuperation. Paul was healed by the Spirit of Christ.

For Paul Christ was not some amorphous, abstract spiritual idea. Rather, Paul was nursed back to health by people who were filled with the Spirit of Christ. It wasn't that some healer laid hands on Paul at a worship service, but rather that actual Christians cared for Paul until he recovered his sight.

Paul called himself the foremost sinner because he had been in charge of the campaign to eliminate Christianity from the face of the earth. Paul's sin was not like what we think of as sin today. Paul was not a thief, not a drunkard or a gambler, and certainly not irresponsible. Rather, Paul had been an upstanding member of the Jewish community, an honored elder statesman, and a trusted confidant of the High Priest. From the community perspective, Paul had the highest trust and integrity. He was an esteemed leader of his community. But in the light of Christ he saw himself as the foremost sinner in the world because he "had acted ignorantly in unbelief" (v. 13).

The Lectionary then provides this story of Paul in 1 Timothy as the background for the parable of the lost sheep. Of course, there are two versions of the lost sheep parable: this one in Luke and one in Matthew 18:10-14. They are similar, but also different.

The Matthew parable begins: "See that you do not despise one of these little ones" (Matt. 18:10). What "little ones"? The previous story in Matthew is about Jesus blessing children, so we assume that he was talking about children. But that is an assumption and we have to be careful of our assumptions. The truth is that we are all children of God irrespective of our age. I am still my parents child regardless of my age. We are all children of God forever.

Matthew was telling us not to overlook insignificant people—children—or to consider anyone to be insignificant because all people have significance in Christ. So, the first point of the Matthew version is that God will go to any lengths to save anyone, anywhere, anytime.

The second point of the Matthew version is that we are all lost sheep. For the most part lost sheep don't think of themselves as being lost. Sheep are simply caught up in the adventure of life, feeding on new grass and chasing butterflies. Sheep have poor eyesight and are fairly unaware, unconcerned, and naturally stupid. They are the opposite of cunning.

The Matthew story was told to the disciples and people generally. Whereas the Luke story was told to the Pharisees. Same story, different audience. In the story the one lost sheep is one of a hundred. A flock of a hundred would have been large. Here the setting of the story is for the prosperous, the Pharisees. He mentions the size of the flock because He is talking to people who have a hundred sheep—Pharisees. Because if you had a flock of a hundred sheep, that was a lot of sheep, which would mean that you were well off.

You were richer than the average person. A flock of a hundred sheep would have been large.

And so the setting here is for the prosperous people, and specifically for the Pharisees. He challenged the Pharisees to care for every sheep in the flock and not to ignore any of them that happened to be lost. If you had a hundred and you miss in one you might think, well, *that's not so much.* He was also telling the Pharisees that finding the lost sheep would require a lot more work for the shepherd. But it will also produce a lot more joy in heaven.

He said that the righteous sheep of the flock don't need a shepherd. And who are the righteous sheep in the flock? Are there any righteous sheep in the flock? A righteous sheep would be aware, concerned, and smart. But sheep are none of these things. And that is the point! The reason that righteous sheep don't need the shepherd is there is no such thing as a righteous sheep.

Years ago a Jewish Rabbi wrote a book called: *Why do bad things happen to good people?* He wrote it because people have struggled over that issue. The answer to his question seems fairly simple to me: There are no good people! Bad things happen to everybody.

Luke's story of the lost sheep provides a message for the shepherds, the leaders, to do the hard work of going out and finding the lost sheep. Because sheep are social animals the rest of the flock will be fine. The shepherd's job is to keep the sheep together. And the one that is lost needs special attention. So, go spend your time finding the lost sheep.

Luke's parable of the lost coin carries the same message. The message is not just for shepherds. It's for everyone, even women. We all must be involved in finding what has been lost, whether sheep or coins. But again it was told for a different audience. This time the message is not just for shepherds. It is a message for everyone. We all must be involved in this project.

So why do the angels rejoice over finding the lost sheep or the lost coin more so than the others? Because the reality is that we are all lost sinners, and the only way into the kingdom of heaven is through the door of repentance, through the door of Jesus Christ. All Christians were formally lost in one way or another. So being a

Christian always involves a change of heart or a change of mind. And for some of us that may have happened so long ago that we've forgotten about it. Nonetheless, we are not what we used to be, nor are we what we will yet be in Christ. We are a people in transition. We are a work in progress. All of us.

Thank you, Jesus. We thank you, Lord, for sending Jesus. We thank you, Jesus, for your insertion into our lives. We are grateful for that. We are not the people we used to be. We know that. But do not fill us with pride because of that. Keep us humble because we are not the people that we need to be, either. We're still working on it, Lord, with your help, through the dispensation of your Holy Spirit.

We are grateful for this church, and for her long history. Though it has been a rocky history, two steps forward and one step back. But we thank you for it all. We pray that you would help us to continue to be as faithful as we can in the midst of a world gone mad. And help us to learn from our mistakes.

We pray for an outpouring of your spirit. Not just here. Of course, we pray for it here, but we pray for it to be not just here. Pour out your grace and mercy throughout the community, throughout the valley, throughout the state, throughout the nation, throughout the world. We need what all of your people need—your guidance, your love, your trust, that relationship with you upon which we can depend.

So, help us to practice living in your light, the light of Christ. Help us to look to you for guidance, and help us to understand that the best place that you give guidance is in your Word, in Scripture. Help us to read your Scripture with understanding, and open our hearts as we pray to the Holy Spirit, that you would give us wisdom and insight with regard to your Word. Because so often your Scripture and your Word provide things that we really don't want to hear. We know that your truth is true, but we also find it hard to bear sometimes. It has a sharp edge. It has a point. So help us to endure the sharp edge of your Truth. Help us to receive that, to rejoice in that. Because you have provided it for our own good, our own growth, our own maturity.

Help us also not to be self-centered, Father, either as individuals or as a church. Help us to remember that we are to be in service to you. We are to wait upon you like a waiter waits a table, anticipating your every concern, Father. Help us not to wait for the end of the world, like we're waiting for a bus. But help us to wait on you to provide what you want for us, as best we're able. Because you do provide what we need.

We thank you, Father, and ask you to continue to provide for our needs. Bless us by helping us to be a blessing to others, and be with us. In the name of Jesus Christ. Amen.

October 11, 2022

Shrewd

1First of all, then, I urge that supplications, prayers, intercessions, and thanksgivings be made for all people, 2 for kings and all who are in high positions, that we may lead a peaceful and quiet life, godly and dignified in every way. 3 This is good, and it is pleasing in the sight of God our Savior, 4 who desires all people to be saved and to come to the knowledge of the truth. 5 For there is one God, and there is one mediator between God and men, the man Christ Jesus, 6 who gave himself as a ransom for all, which is the testimony given at the proper time. 7 For this I was appointed a preacher and an apostle (I am telling the truth, I am not lying), a teacher of the Gentiles in faith and truth.

—1 Timothy 2:1-7

He also said to the disciples, "There was a rich man who had a manager, and charges were brought to him that this man was wasting his possessions. 2 And he called him and said to him, 'What is this that I hear about you? Turn in the account of your management, for you can no longer be manager.' 3 And the manager said to himself, 'What shall I do, since my master is taking the management away from me? I am not strong enough to dig, and I am ashamed to beg. 4 I have decided what to do, so that when I am removed from management, people may receive me into their houses.' 5 So, summoning his master's debtors one by one, he said to the first, 'How much do you owe my master?' 6 He said, 'A hundred measures of oil.' He said to him, 'Take your bill, and sit down quickly and write fifty.' 7 Then he said to another, 'And how much do you owe?' He said, 'A hundred measures of wheat.' He said to him, 'Take your bill, and write eighty.' 8 The master commended the dishonest manager for his shrewdness.

For the sons of this world are more shrewd in dealing with their own generation than the sons of light. 9 And I tell you, make friends for yourselves by means of unrighteous wealth, so that when it fails they may receive you into the eternal dwellings. 10 "One who is faithful in a very little is also faithful in much, and one who is dishonest in a very little is also dishonest in much. 11 If then you have not been faithful in the unrighteous wealth, who will entrust to you the true riches? 12 And if you have not been faithful in that which is another's, who will give you that which is your own? 13 No servant can serve two masters, for either he will hate the one and love the other, or he will be devoted to the one and despise the other. You cannot serve God and money." —*Luke 16:1-13*

Paul urged Christians to pray for all people, "that supplications, prayers, intercessions, and thanksgivings be made for all people" (1 Timothy 2:1). *All* people! What is a supplication? It is a petition, an earnest or humble request. And to whom is a supplication made? To to a superior authority. A supplication is a formal request for a right or benefit from a person or group in authority. It is a formal request seeking a court's intervention and action on a matter.

And what are Christians to ask the court for? For prayers, where prayers are understood to be a wish, expressed as a petition to God, to God's court. Our prayers are to ask for the fulfillment of an obligation, a prayer, a vow. And what is to be the content or meaning of our prayers. We are to ask the court, to ask God, for His intercession with reference to the petitions of believers to fall in line with God's will. By asking God to intervene, we are asking the church, the body of Christ, believers, to intervene according to God's will.

Paul was telling us how the one intervening should get involved after drawing near to God and agreeing with His revealed will. True intercession seeks to act only as the Lord directs. Christians are to follow His will, to act as His hands extended into the world. In this case we are to plead on another's behalf for all parties involved.

Christians are to intervene in the affairs of others in order to express God's will. Make no mistake, Christians are to meddle in the lives of others on behalf of God because God is meddling in the life of the world in order to provide salvation. God has to meddle, has to insert Himself in people's lives because unsaved people don't want God's help. And salvation requires His help. It cannot be done apart from God.

God has sent Jesus Christ to meddle in the affairs of the world, to intrude into other people's affairs or business, to interfere with our plans, our hopes and dreams for our future. Why does God do this? For what purpose does He meddle? Paul was praying for a particular group of people: "for kings and all who are in high positions" (1 Timothy 2:2). He was not aiming at regular people here. He was aiming at the leaders of society.

God has a gift for those who will receive it. At the time that Paul wrote, those who accepted the gospel were ordinary people at best. Most were slaves, commoners, and an assortment of social misfits and outcasts. It would be hundreds of years before the gospel penetrated to the higher echalons of society. Nonetheless, it is a gift of eternal value, inestimable worth—salvation from hell and damnation.

Paul was praying for these people, the leaders of society, because they were unreached. They wanted nothing to do with Jesus or His gospel. And while they were yet unsaved, Paul prayed that Christians would be thankful for them. Christians are to be grateful, thankful, and full of appreciation "for kings and all who are in high positions" (1 Timothy 2:2), even when they are unsaved. Why would Paul want Christians to be thankful for people who were not saved, especially for unsaved people who were responsible for causing much harm to fellow Christians?

Today Christians are again in the same situation, in that the leaders of the world in 2022 are not only overwhelmingly not Christian, but are in increasing opposition to Christianity. So, Paul's prayer is for us today. Paul prayed that kings and social leaders would join the ranks of Christians and "lead a peaceful and quiet life, godly and dignified in every way" (1 Timothy 2:2).

And because the unsaved are unable to lead such lives, unable to even understand the value of such living, Christians are to model this behavior for them. In the midst of difficulty, persecution, trial, and tribulation, Christians are to model a peaceful, quiet, dignified life in Christ as a means of evangelism. Evangelism is not just telling people about Jesus, evangelism is showing people the power of Christ by living quietly in the midst of chaos, by living honestly in the midst of fraud and deceit, by living courageously in the midst of cowardly avoidance of speaking God's truth.

We are to pray for *all* people, and especially for kings and leaders to lead quiet and peaceful lives. However, peace and the lack of conflict are not the same thing. The only real power is peace. Practicing peace requires patience and discipline. The lack of conflict is just the absence of peace. You can't pursue the lack of conflict, because the lack of something not something real. The lack of something is not a thing. It is no-thing. You can only pursue peace, which requires positive, disciplined action. It doesn't mean "don't fight." It means to actively pursue mutual understanding and what is good for others. It means doing what is best for them, but not what *we* think is best for them. It means doing what *God* thinks is best for them.

To be quiet literally means keeping one's seat, and by implication, being still, undisturbed, not disturbing others, being peaceable (able to keep the peace), being at rest. But not asleep! Being quiet means being even-tempered, unflappable, consistent, balanced. It means being a Godly person, who has shown an inner response to the things of God. Being quiet shows itself in godly piety or reverence, having a humble heart-response that naturally expresses itself in reverence for God, and the things of God.

Paul also tells Christians to be dignified, to respect what deserves due reverence, what has a sense of gravity and invites reverence. Being dignified means respect for what is august, venerable, and time-honored. It means having the kind of respectability that reflects what has been transformed by God and exhibits moral and spiritual *gravitas.* Dignity reveals a deep, godly character that honors what is noble and morally elevated.

Paul will further explain all of these things in 1 Timothy 3 & 4, where he discusses the qualifications for deacons and elders; church leadership. But these things are not just for church deacons and elders as office holders. They are for all Christians. These things describe the ideal inner life of faithful Christians. Of course, church leaders need to be, first of all, faithful Christians because the real job of all church leaders is to model faithfulness, to simply be faithful, to be ordinary Christians. Not average Christians, but ordinary Christians, where *ordinary* means conformity in quality or kind with the regular order of things, and in this case the regular or regulated order of God as found in the Bible. Being a faithful Christian should be ordinary, common, and familiar. Simply being faithful is the real solution to all of the world's problems. What if faithfulness was common? The world would be very different. That's the goal.

All of this discussion in 1 Timothy sets up the parable of the dishonest manager in Luke 16 where Jesus' audience includes disciples and Pharisees, those charged with church management and community leadership. Just as Paul prayed for "kings and all who are in high positions" (1 Timothy 2:2), Jesus aimed His remarks at the Pharisees. The story is an accusation of mismanagement, of dereliction of duty, of failure to do the job. Jesus was talking to the Pharisees, but the disciples were also in view.

Luke 15, the parable of the lost sheep, the lost coin, and the prodigal son, reveals the Pharisees' motivation. They were lovers of money and justified themselves before men and exalted that which was an abomination before God. They were not faithful to the teachings of the Old Testament.

Luke 16 then tells about the dishonest manager or steward. He knew that he wouldn't find another job, so he acted in his own interest by ingratiating people to him. His job was to collect debts for his boss. But knowing that he had lost favor with his boss, he reduced the amount of the debt he would collect. It was an apparent act of mercy on his part, but it wasn't his money. Scripture doesn't say that the debts were paid off because of the reduction. He didn't have the authority to do what he did. Or if they were paid off, to whom would the money go. We don't know if the dishonest manager then gave all he collected to his boss, or whether he just kept it for himself, knowing that he had been fired. The point of the story is that the manager acted on his own initiative for his own behalf. He was shrewd. He showed initiative, selfish though it was.

A shrewd person has personal insight. To be shrewd is to be smart, to scheme. Shred means having or showing clever awareness or resourcefulness, especially in practical matters, taking personal initiative, being bright and resourceful. It means using effective and cunning practices, being tricky, sharp, penetrating, and smart. Jesus' point was: *don't be stupid.* He used the words *shrewd* and *cunning* fifty-four times in the New Testament.

"Behold, I am sending you out as sheep in the midst of wolves, so be wise as serpents and innocent as doves" (Matthew 10:16).

Jesus wants Christians be be shrewd without being dishonest or unfaithful. Becoming *homo Christos* is not a denial of our *homo sapien*-ness. We are to have both wisdom and innocence. Being faithful is not the renunciation of intelligence or academics. It sometimes seems that Christian fundamentalists are opposed to intelligence and academics, probably because Liberalism comes out of academia, and liberals like to think that they are better than other people. And fundamentalists are rightly opposed to that. Biblical criticism originated in the universities, and much of it in the German and American Evangelical churches in the 1800s. It's not all bad; it's not all liberal. There is a faithful strain of biblical academics.

"Now the serpent was more crafty than any other beast of the field that the Lord God had made" (Genesis 3:1).

Being innocent does not mean being gullible. Original sin is reliance on human wisdom, but the solution to the problem is not human stupidity. It is not the renunciation of human wisdom. Rather, it is a matter of getting our priorities straight. Human wisdom does not trump God. Wisdom is a good thing, but not when it is divorced from God.

"Hear, O Israel: The Lord our God, the Lord is one" (Deuteronomy 6:4).

The *Shema* (Deuteronomy 6:4) means that God is first. It is not just about the unity of God, but is also about the priority of God.

Human wisdom is a good thing, but it does not supersede God's Word.

"And I tell you, make friends for yourselves by means of unrighteous wealth, so that when it fails they may receive you into the eternal dwellings" (Luke 16:9).

Money, like power, corrupts. The more money one has, the more one is exposed to corruption. Having money is not a bad thing. The bad thing is hording money, failing to be generous. Money in-and-of-itself is not evil. It is a necessity in this world. Jesus was telling his disciples to be gracious to *all* people, even the rich, in spite of their wealth.

"First of all, then, I urge that supplications, prayers, intercessions, and thanksgivings be made for all people" (1 Timothy 2:1).

Graciousness begets graciousness; kindness begets kindness. Smile at others and they generally smile back. Bark at others and they will bark at you. Being faithful means being gracious and kind. Yet, faithful, gracious, kind people get taken advantage of. They do! So, knowing that we can be taken advantage of, we must not be stupid. But neither are we to avoid the hard consequences of being faithful, gracious, and kind. Be faithful, but be smart about it. But don't let your wisdom trump your faithfulness.

You *will* suffer for being faithful, gracious, and kind. Do it anyway. Suffering is a common consequence of faithfulness. Nonetheless, we need to do what we can to minimize our suffering, so that we can maximize our faithfulness. Suffering is a consequence of sensitivity, response-ability, and love. Suffering reveals God. Suffering connects us to God. As Queen Elizabeth said: "Grief is the price we pay for love." Lord, make us faithful. Amen.

September 18, 2022

CONFESSION/PROFESSION

6 But godliness with contentment is great gain, 7 for we brought
nothing into the world, and we cannot take anything out of the
world. 8 But if we have food and clothing, with these we will be con-
tent. 9 But those who desire to be rich fall into temptation, into a
snare, into many senseless and harmful desires that plunge people into
ruin and destruction. 10 For the love of money is a root of all kinds
of evils. It is through this craving that some have wandered away
from the faith and pierced themselves with many pangs. 11 But as for
you, O man of God, flee these things. Pursue righteousness, godliness,
faith, love, steadfastness, gentleness. 12 Fight the good fight of the
faith. Take hold of the eternal life to which you were called and about
which you made the good confession in the presence of many wit-
nesses. 13 I charge you in the presence of God, who gives life to all
things, and of Christ Jesus, who in his testimony before Pontius Pi-
late made the good confession, 14 to keep the commandment un-
stained and free from reproach until the appearing of our Lord Jesus
Christ, 15 which he will display at the proper time—he who is the
blessed and only Sovereign, the King of kings and Lord of lords, 16
who alone has immortality, who dwells in unapproachable light,
whom no one has ever seen or can see. To him be honor and eternal
dominion. Amen. —*1 Timothy 6:6-16*

19 "There was a rich man who was clothed in purple and fine linen
and who feasted sumptuously every day. 20 And at his gate was laid
a poor man named Lazarus, covered with sores, 21 who desired to be
fed with what fell from the rich man's table. Moreover, even the dogs
came and licked his sores. 22 The poor man died and was carried by

the angels to Abraham's side. The rich man also died and was buried,
23 and in Hades, being in torment, he lifted up his eyes and saw
Abraham far off and Lazarus at his side. 24 And he called out, 'Fa-
ther Abraham, have mercy on me, and send Lazarus to dip the end of
his finger in water and cool my tongue, for I am in anguish in this
flame.' 25 But Abraham said, 'Child, remember that you in your life-
time received your good things, and Lazarus in like manner bad
things; but now he is comforted here, and you are in anguish. 26 And
besides all this, between us and you a great chasm has been fixed, in
order that those who would pass from here to you may not be able,
and none may cross from there to us.' 27 And he said, 'Then I beg
you, father, to send him to my father's house— 28 for I have five
brothers—so that he may warn them, lest they also come into this
place of torment.' 29 But Abraham said, 'They have Moses and the
Prophets; let them hear them.' 30 And he said, 'No, father Abraham,
but if someone goes to them from the dead, they will repent.' 31 He
said to him, 'If they do not hear Moses and the Prophets, neither will
they be convinced if someone should rise from the dead.'"

—Luke 16:19-31

What is "Godliness with contentment" (1 Timothy 6:6)? Godliness is simply the discipline of faithfulness. Godliness is God-likeness. Godliness is Christian discipline and faithfulness. It is just ordinary faithfulness. But it takes discipline and practice. Godliness does not require great accomplishments, only simple faithfulness. To be Godly is to exercise the fruits of the spirit in one's own life—love, joy, peace, patience, kindness, goodness, faithfulness, gentleness, and self-control. It is the result of the work of the Holy Spirit in a Christian's life.

This is the life-giving and sustaining fruit (food) that the world needs. It's not up to other people to provide it, it's up to Christians, to us! Godliness is simple faithfulness. And as easy as that is to say, it is a lot more difficult to do than most people would imagine. Paul contrasted the acts of the flesh:

"sexual immorality, impurity, sensuality, idolatry, sorcery, enmity, strife, jealousy, fits of anger, rivalries, dissensions, divisions, envy, drunkenness, orgies, and things like these (Galatians 5:19),

to the good fruit of the Spirit:

> *"love, joy, peace, patience, kindness, goodness, faithfulness, gentleness, self-control" (Galatians 5:22-23).*

This is the fruit that God is looking for, the fruit that is to emerge from His church, from His people.

And of course, these are the works of the Holy Spirit who comes and renews us. We are unable to do these things on our own, apart from the Holy Spirit, because we do not want to. We would rather do our own stuff. So the Holy Spirit comes and changes what it is that we want. After the Holy Spirit changes us we then want to please God.

This fruit of the spirit is the life-giving food, the sustaining fruit that the world needs, that the world is clamoring for, that the world is starved for. But the thing for us to understand is that it is not for other people to produce this fruit for the world. It is up to *us!* We need to produce it for our own friends and family in our own communities. And in as much as everybody begins doing that, there will be plenty in the world.

Paul instructed Timothy to beware of the temptation of wealth. Why is money a temptation? Because it gives people the ability and the opportunity to do whatever they want. If you have the money, you can do whatever you want. And that throws us back into original sin. Original sin in the garden was Adam and Eve doing what *they* wanted in spite of what God had told them. Apart from Christ we never escape the temptation and devastation of original sin. Paul said,

> *"O man of God, flee these things. Pursue righteousness, godliness, faith, love, steadfastness, gentleness. Fight the good fight of the faith. Take hold of the eternal life to which you were called and about which you made the good confession in the presence of many witnesses" (1 Timothy 6:11-12).*

Take hold of eternal life. He's telling Timothy, right in the present moment, to take hold of the eternal life. Do it now! It's like if I were to say to, *take hold of eternal life right now while you are in the pew.* That is interesting because it teaches that our eternal life in Christ has already begun. We don't have to wait to get to heaven. We're in it right now if we are in Christ, but only in Christ. Of course, we're not completely in it. We've got one foot in it. We are moving in that direction. But the point is that eternal life is real, and available right now. Eternal life has already begun! It is ours to realize, our work is to conform to the reality of eternal life on earth.

Then Paul said, "keep the commandment" (v. 14). What commandment? He doesn't say what commandment to keep. There are ten of them, and the Pharisees had hundreds. So what commandment was he talking about? Jesus was asked this question by the rich, young ruler. And Jesus said, *love God first, love neighbor second, and then love self third.* This, then sets up the story of the rich man and Lazarus in the Luke.

It's a story about eternal life, about heaven and hell. The rich man was a child of Abraham, a Jew. And so was Lazarus. Both were Jews so it's a family story. And the shocking thing was that not all Jews would be in heaven. This ran counter to the common Jewish belief at the time. In the story there is a great distinction between these two Jews. And that should give us pause. In order to understand this, we turn to Romans 9:

> *"6 But it is not as though the word of God has failed. For not all who are descended from Israel belong to Israel, and not all are children of Abraham because they are his offspring, but 'Through Isaac shall your offspring be named.' This means that it is not the children of the flesh who are the children of God, but the children of the promise are counted as offspring. For this is what the promise said: 'About this time next year I will return, and Sarah shall have a son.' And not only so, but also when Rebekah had conceived children by one man, our forefather Isaac, though they were not yet born and had done nothing either good or bad—in order that God's purpose of election might continue, not because of works but because of him who calls—she was told, 'The older will serve the younger'" (Romans 9:6-12).*

Paul said that all Jews are not Abraham's children, the children of God's promise to Abraham. And today the same thing can be said of

Christianity: not all Christians, not all church members, are of Christ. If this does not disturb you, then you have not understood it! Jesus said the same thing, and He said it before Paul. Paul was simply repeating the idea he got from Jesus.

> *"Not everyone who says to me, 'Lord, Lord,' will enter the kingdom of heaven, but the one who does the will of my Father who is in heaven. On that day many will say to me, 'Lord, Lord, did we not prophesy in your name, and cast out demons in your name, and do many mighty works in your name?' And then will I declare to them, 'I never knew you; depart from me, you workers of lawlessness'" (Matthew 7:21-23).*

Jesus was speaking to church leaders! Those who prophesied, cast out demons, and did mighty works were church leaders of some sort. So, what was Jesus' problem with them? It takes more than calling on Jesus to be a Christian. What was missing was their confession. They were doing the work of leadership in their own strength. They were directing the Spirit, not being directed by the Spirit. They thought of themselves as faithful, but Christ did not.

We don't make ourselves Christian by thinking ourselves to be Christian, nor does confession alone make people Christian. We may have said the right words, signed the right documents, joined the right church, maybe even thought the right thoughts. But apart from Christ's acknowledgment, people are not Christian in reality.

Our confession is necessary, but inadequate. It's kind of like a TV show or movie, where a crime has been committed by a wife or a child, perhaps a murder. And the loving husband or the loving mother then confesses to the crime in order to protect the child from the consequences of the law. But in the end there is no proof of the viability of the false confession. It turns out that the confession is proven to be a lie. Similarly, God requires proof of our confession of Christ. And our lives of simple, ordinary fruitful faithfulness is the proof of our faith, which Christ then confirms. That's the proof that God is looking for.

Our words are not trustworthy. People can say all sorts of things that are not true. So, you and I by ourselves cannot provide the proof that God requires because our testimony is unreliable. Our word is not trustworthy. So, God sent His Son to do what we cannot do. And in doing so Jesus died on the cross for our sin—because of our sinfulness. And to keep us from idolizing the human Jesus, He sent the Holy Spirit to guide and direct us individually, personally. God's Holy Spirit has been dispatched into our lives, our hearts, our minds. And God trusts His Holy Spirit to speak the truth. So the Holy Spirit provides our profession of faith. God's Holy Spirit is one with God's Word, the Bible. Consequently, if you don't know the Bible, you can't know God's will.

Confession is necessary but not sufficient. Profession must be added. To confess is to admit, to "fess up." Admit what? Our sinfulness, our weakness, our faults, our particular sins. Confession must be particular, not general. We must name our sins.

The prefix *con* means *with*, and *pro* means *ahead of time*, or *in advance*. So with *con*fession we acknowledge our inability to save ourselves. We acknowledge our inability to think right, to be right, to be fully human. We must understand our own weaknesses and our own sin. That is our *con*fession, so we must admit that.

*Pro*fession, then, is more of a vow, more of a promise. It is a declaration, openly and publicly made. With profession we make a promise about our future behavior, our future condition. Profession, then, requires confession, but profession is more than confession. We confess our inability, and we profess Christ's ability. We profess not only our own promise, but we profess Christ's promise to deliver His people from sin. We confess our lack of the Holy Spirit, our failure to live in obedience to the Holy Spirit, and then we profess the presence of the Holy Spirit in our lives. We profess His power to change us, as we confess our lack of power to change ourselves. And this is not a contradiction.

There was a time before our regeneration (confession), and a time after our regeneration (profession). God's Holy Spirit is the glue that holds it all together, that unites us with Christ. The Spirit in God recognizes the Spirit in Jesus Christ. And the Spirit in Jesus Christ recognizes the Spirit in His people. And the Spirit in me recognizes the Spirit in you. We are not Christian apart from all of this mutual recognition. The Holy Spirit recognizes Himself in all of this. And the Holy Spirit is the authority.

And so we recognize one another as Christians. You may have seen this mutual recognition in operation. Have you ever gone to a place where you don't know anybody, and you strike up a conversation with a stranger and discover they are Christian. Christians have an uncanny ability to recognize other Christians. There is a family resemblance in their behavior. To re-cognize is to be mindful of, to be respectfully aware of something or someone.

Thus, people are not truly Christian until and unless they recognize God's Holy Spirit in their own lives, and are recognized by the Holy Spirit, in God, in Christ, and in one another. People are not truly Christian until and unless they/we are aware of God, and God is aware of them/us, until we are aware that we know God in a real way; and we know that God knows that we know. All of this recognition and knowing is spiritual confirmation.

Herein lies the real unity of Christ's church: mutual recognition of Father, Son, and Holy Spirit in one another, in you and in me. This is the unity that Jesus prayed for: John 17:20-22:

> *"I do not ask for these only, but also for those who will believe in me through their word, that they may all be one, just as you, Father, are in me, and I in you, that they also may be in us, so that the world may believe that you have sent me. The glory that you have given me I have given to them, that they may be one even as we are one"*

This Church unity is not a bunch of officials getting together and trying to agree on some statement of faith. We've tried that for a thousand years, and it hasn't worked very well. Church unity is you and I recognizing the Holy Spirit in one another and in others. And that is sufficient! Praise be to God!

Lord, we are so grateful for your presence in our lives, for your presence in this church, in our lives over the decades in this church, actually over the centuries. And we give you thanks for that. We've had our ups, we've had our downs individually and corporately. So help us to be who you have called us to be, give us the vision to see it and understand it clearly, and then give us the courage to walk it out in our lives.

And help us to know that you are not calling us to greatness, you are actually calling us to ordinariness. You're just looking for ordinary people to be ordinary Christians in their ordinary lives. And what a difference that would make in our world if that was common, if even half of the people were simply ordinary Christians. And so we pray for *that,* Father.

We know that you are bringing the kingdom here on earth as it is in heaven. And yet this world is so far away from your kingdom. There's not a lot that we can do as we watch the news on TV and see all the stuff that's going on. What is happening in the news is mostly outside of our authority or relationships. So help us to not get caught up in that. But help us to focus on the actual relationships that we have, our family and friends, local people, people that are real to us, people that we can make a difference with, that we have some ability to affect.

And help us to know that we don't have to go out and browbeat people with the Bible. If we simply lift up your faithfulness, Lord, if we simply be ordinary Christians in the midst of a world gone mad, people will take note, and they will ask us why we seem to be different. Then we can talk to them because they are willing to listen.

And so we pray for this world, we pray for those who don't seem to know you, though we know that in the back of their minds they do. We pray that you would dispatch your Holy Spirit to change their hearts and minds. We can't change hearts and minds. We know that. But you can. And we know that because you have changed our hearts and minds. And so we pray for *that*, Father, that you would dispatch your Holy Spirit to do His work in our world.

Of course, we know also that He works through us, so it's not going to happen apart from us. It's going to happen through us, a little bit here and there, now and then, as best we're able. So help us Father, to do that, to do what we can, and to be who you have made us to be.

And we pray for this sin torn world. We pray against the war that's raging, the wars that have raged forever. We pray against those who encourage warfare. We pray for peace, but we also know that the only peace that is real is the peace of Jesus Christ. Make it so, Father. Amen.

October 25, 2022

Duty

8 Do not be ashamed of the testimony about our Lord, nor of me his
prisoner, but share in suffering for the gospel by the power of God, 9
who saved us and called us to a holy calling, not because of our
works but because of his own purpose and grace, which he gave us in
Christ Jesus before the ages began, 10 and which now has been manifested through the appearing of our Savior Christ Jesus, who abolished death and brought life and immortality to light through the
gospel, 11 for which I was appointed a preacher and apostle and
teacher, 12 which is why I suffer as I do. But I am not ashamed, for I
know whom I have believed, and I am convinced that he is able to
guard until that day what has been entrusted to me. 13 Follow the
pattern of the sound words that you have heard from me, in the faith
and love that are in Christ Jesus. 14 By the Holy Spirit who dwells
within us, guard the good deposit entrusted to you.

—2 Timothy 1:8-14

5 The apostles said to the Lord, "Increase our faith!" 6 And the Lord
said, "If you had faith like a grain of mustard seed, you could say to
this mulberry tree, 'Be uprooted and planted in the sea,' and it would
obey you. 7 "Will any one of you who has a servant plowing or
keeping sheep say to him when he has come in from the field, 'Come
at once and recline at table'? 8 Will he not rather say to him, 'Prepare
supper for me, and dress properly, and serve me while I eat and drink,
and afterward you will eat and drink'? 9 Does he thank the servant
because he did what was commanded? 10 So you also, when you
have done all that you were commanded, say, 'We are unworthy servants; we have only done what was our duty.'"

—Luke 17:5-10

Again, this is a difficult scripture to deal with, partly because Luke tells us that we have a duty. And duty in today's world has fallen on hard times. People don't like duty. They don't think much of duty. None of us think highly of the word *duty*. It has become a negative word in the world and in the church. So what is duty?

Duty is an act or a course of action that is required of one by position, social custom, law, or religion. To have a duty is to be bound to do something. It sounds like works-righteousness, and it can be, but not necessarily. Works-righteousness is a form of self-righteousness that believes that salvation can be earned by doing good works, that we can make ourselves righteous before God by our obedience. The logic is that if we do good works, then God owes us a salvation. In a way we can make ourselves righteous before God by engaging in good works, by being obedient to God. And of course, this was the religion of the Pharisees. This is what they thought.

Jesus reserved for the Pharisees His harshest criticism. He called them whitewashed tombs and hypocrites. Why would He call them that? Because they had misunderstood the gospel of salvation.

We do not deserve salvation. We have no right to expect it. It does not come because of our works. It does not come because of our obedience. Rather, it comes to us because of what Christ did on the cross. In a sense, I suppose you could say it is the works of Christ that brought us salvation. And that's not wrong. Nonetheless, it is not our own works that saves us.

In an attempt to avoid the dangers of works-righteousness, many evangelicals go to the other extreme, something theologians call antinomianism. This doctrine argues that if obedience to God's law does not save me, then it's just not that important. So the church in our day, in an effort to avoid the dangers of works-righteousness, we find that many Christians and evangelicals have gone to the other extreme: antinomianism. *Anti* means *against,* and *nom* means *law*. It's a Latin term. It means against the law or opposed to the law.

Antinomianism argues that obedience to God's law does not save people. And that's correct. Therefore, they mistakenly conclude that

God's law is not important. That's incorrect. Antinomians correctly believe that grace provides an unearned ticket to heaven. So they think that they are good to go. *I got my ticket, my salvation to heaven right here in my pocket, so it doesn't really matter what I do while I'm waiting for God's bus.* This is the "bus ticket to heaven syndrome." *My salvation is my ticket to heaven, and what I do on earth while I wait for the bus, good or bad, doesn't matter. I have my ticket, I'm good.*

But that's not entirely true. Tim Keller, a pastor in New York, said, a lot of people think, *I obey, therefore I'm accepted*. But the gospel says, *I'm accepted, therefore I obey*. The order of these things is important. In fact, obedience is really important. The gospel does not nullify our obedience to God's Word. It does not eliminate our duty to be obedient. Obedience is still a duty.

In true Christianity, faith always and necessarily expresses itself in action. Martin Luther and John Calvin said that while good works could not merit salvation, they do prove or reveal or show or demonstrate the genuineness of our faith. So we are saved by faith alone, but the faith that saves us is never alone. This might seem to be confusing, but it really isn't. The saving faith that is true is always accompanied by good works, by obedience to God. Good works are not just what we do at church, and they are not just going out and doing acts of evangelism.

Rather, our good works are to encompass everything that we do in our churches, our communities, our families, our homes, our jobs, our employees, our hobbies—everything we do. All of these areas should be affected by our faith. And in today's world, there are too many Christians who are deceived into thinking that people who live immorally can still enjoy the righteousness of Christ because salvation is by grace alone. They think that because God forgives sin (and He does), therefore God doesn't care about sin, but He does. The first half of that is true. He does forgive sin, but he also cares about it. He doesn't want us to sin.

Part of the confusion comes from the term *works-righteousness* because that term is used on both sides of the argument. On the one hand, works cannot save you, but on the other, works are necessary. Even if we say that works are necessary, but not sufficient, we still get the cart before the horse. Works, faithful action, faithful deeds, are the product of faith, the result, not the cause. Grace and works go together. Grace results in works, but works cannot produce faith. So, if you don't have faith and you think that good works can produce faith, you're sadly mistaken. It doesn't work that way. You can work all you want, and it just won't get you there because without faith you don't really *want* the Lord. You're just trying to manipulate Him.

So an alternative term that we might use to help us out is to think of it as *law-righteousness* as opposed to *works-righteousness*. Salvation does not come by law-righteousness. We can't make ourselves righteous by obeying the law. Our actions do not cause God to provide His grace. Even if we follow God's law to the letter, even if we're actually saved, we still never measure up to God's standard.

The reason that faithfulness to God's law cannot produce true righteousness is that faithfulness to God's law is impossible apart from regeneration by the Holy Spirit. Before or apart from regeneration, human motives are self-centered. After regeneration or with the guidance of the Holy Spirit human motives become Christ-centered. Not perfectly, but adequately; not all at once, but over time, bit by bit we grow in grace, and mature in faithfulness.

Paul told Timothy that he was Christ's prisoner, not Rome's prisoner. Paul was a willing prisoner of Christ, a willing bondservant of the Lord, a willing slave to Christ Jesus. Paul was an example of a saved Christian, and we are to emulate Paul in this regard. Paul was not embarrassed or ashamed to be a slave to Christ. He also said that the reason for his slavery to Christ was his love of Christ.

> *"By the Holy Spirit who dwells within us, guard the good deposit entrusted to you." (2 Timothy 1: 14).*

Paul was a prisoner to Christ because the Holy Spirit was dwelling in him. So when Paul became a Christian, he realized that he had previously been a slave to sin. So now, in Christ he was no longer a slave to sin. He now claimed to be a slave to Jesus Christ. And that's really interesting because he's still a slave. But in Christ he becomes a willing slave to Jesus Christ.

The dispatching of the Holy Spirit to Paul and to us, is a down payment. Jesus Christ has made a down payment for possession of humanity. God has made a down payment for humanity. The down payment has given God ownership control. Ownership is being transferred as the Holy Spirit grows and matures in us, and as the Holy Spirit reaches others. It's already a done deal, but it is not yet complete. It's just a matter of time.

Consider buying a house. To get the ownership of the house you have to give the previous owner the total price. And you are not the owner until you get the total price over to the former owner. For us banks are involved. We get a loan from the bank and we give a little bit of money for the house, and the bank gives the rest. The down payment is just a little of what it's going to take to buy the house. So God makes a down payment by dispatching his Holy Spirit to us. He gives the whole spirit, but we can't handle it all at once, so we get a little of it. And over time, it grows. Over time, regular small payments are made. And at the end of the process, we belong fully to God as individuals and eventually as humanity. Paul is an example of all of that.

Another aspect of that down payment is that once you make the down payment, once you start the process, you are then considered to be the owner of the house. Same thing with God. God made the down payment. He is now considered the owner of you, of us, of humanity. The full ownership is being transferred as the Holy Spirit grows and matures in us. And as the Holy Spirit reaches out and touches other people in humanity, He grows. The spirit grows.

The apostles said to the Lord, "Increase our faith!" (Luke 17:5). Jesus told the parable of the mustard seed. The seed is tiny, but the bush grows to be huge. Notice that He was not talking to *an* apostle; he was talking to the apostles, plural. It's not that an individual Christian can be like a mustard seed, but that a community of Christians can do exceedingly great things. Is this true? Science and technology are a fruit of Christianity, and these Christian fruits have given us great power. The community of Christians can do miracles. How can we understand this? Is this even true?

Modern science and technology grew out of Christian Europe. Modern science and technology did not grow out of China. They did not grow out of India. I mention those nations because both China and India have much, much longer histories than Europe. But in Europe, modern science and technology grew and blossomed. Why? There are detailed arguments to be made, but for our purposes here we will simply claim the conclusion that it is because of Christianity, because of God. Modern science and technology are gifts of God. God has given them. And lo and behold, with these gifts, we can move mountains. Literally, it's amazing.

The point is that groups of people can accomplish much more than mere individuals can accomplish. When we work together, we are a lot more powerful than when we work alone. However, with great power, also comes great responsibility. Jesus then put the apostles (and all believers) in God's position. We are bond-servants of God. But what if we owned bond-servants of our own? The parable reverses the order of things by putting us in God's position.

"Will any one of you who has a servant" (v. 7) ask your servant (employee who is working on the clock) to dine with you? Probably not. Rather, you'd tell him or her to do what you are paying them to do. When the work is done, then they can rest. The issue that Jesus raises is: Should the master, the owner of the business, thank employees for doing their jobs?

The point of the story is not the cruelty of the master or his lack of gratitude for good, faithful employees (slaves). This is a difficult idea for us because in our modern world, we want to thank everybody for everything. And I'm not saying that's wrong. Its okay. It's not a bad thing to thank people. But is a business owner obligated to thank employees for doing their jobs?

And when the tables are turned and we are the employee, how should we feel? Should we expect to be thanked for doing what we are paid to do? Again, today we thank people for doing their jobs, doing their duty. And that's OK! But that's not the point the story is making. The story is not about God, it's about us. Do we expect to be thanked for doing our job?

Calvin said of this story:

> "The object of this parable is to show that God claims all that belongs to us as his property, and possesses entire control over our persons and services; and, therefore, that all the zeal that may be manifested by us in discharging our duty does not lay him under obligation to us by any sort of merit; for, as we are his property, so he on his part can owe us nothing."

God owes us nothing. That's the point of grace. If God owes us, then whatever He gives us is not grace. If we think that God owes us anything, any thanks, it is we who are guilty of arrogance, thinking more of ourselves than we should. If we deserve grace, it's not grace. It is our duty to love our husband or wife or children. But if that duty is done with any expectation of something in return, the duty kills the love. It turns our love into a tit-for-tat, a kind of "eye for an eye" exchange. It turns love into a strategy.

Christian love is agape, love without expectation of anything in return. Christian love is charity, generosity that includes freedom from pettiness in character and mind. Christians are obligated to love, bound to love—not as a duty, but as an opportunity, as a joy! We don't love because we have to, or because we are expected to. We love because we want to. Love compels us. We love because we are in the grip of love. In the grip of God's love for us. We are putty in His hands. Or clay; He is the potter, we are the clay.

My mom used to say: *sin is its own punishment*. Similarly, love is its own joy. Our duty is to be joyful in all things, joyful in spite of all things. Can we do that? Let's try!

Heavenly Father, again, we are so blessed because you have dispatched your Holy Spirit, because you have made that down payment not only for us, but for humanity. Not everybody knows that, not everybody realizes that, but your Word says that it's true. Your word says that it's a done deal. Even though it's not complete, the papers have been signed, the down payment has been made, and the installment payments are being made.

We are yours, Father. Help us to know that. Help us to realize that. Help us to make that real. And help us to love that. Help us to love the fact that we are your people. Help us to love the fact that you have given us grace, and given us your love when we don't deserve it. Help us to be changed by your love. Help us to grow into your Holy Spirit. Help us to manifest the fruits of the Spirit, to live by the character of Christ. May His character fill our lives. May we want Him and desire Him more than anything else.

We are grateful, Father, that you brought us together, that we can come together and hear your Word and practice the fruits of your Spirit together. So be with us as we do that. We continue to pray for this church, that you will provide the things that we need, and we know that you have done that in the past, and we trust that you will continue to do that.

Once you get a hold of us, you do not let go. Help us to celebrate that. And yet we know that we are still in this world, and in this flesh, and in the difficulties and troubles of this world. And again, we pray for this war-torn and broken and sinful world, and we pray for those who are for you, and against those who are against you, not against them personally, just against their practices, their beliefs that are not right.

So we pray that you would use the difficulties and problems of this world to accomplish your purposes. And we know that you do that. You have done that in the past, and you are continuing to do that. Again help us to be who you called us to be. Give us the vision, the eyes to see it, and the courage to walk it out in Jesus' name. Amen.

October 2, 2022

As They Went

*8 Remember Jesus Christ, risen from the dead, the offspring of
David, as preached in my gospel, 9 for which I am suffering, bound
with chains as a criminal. But the word of God is not bound! 10
Therefore I endure everything for the sake of the elect, that they also
may obtain the salvation that is in Christ Jesus with eternal glory. 11
The saying is trustworthy, for: If we have died with him, we will
also live with him; 12 if we endure, we will also reign with him; if
we deny him, he also will deny us; 13 if we are faithless, he remains
faithful—for he cannot deny himself. 14 Remind them of these
things, and charge them before God not to quarrel about words, which
does no good, but only ruins the hearers. 15 Do your best to present
yourself to God as one approved, a worker who has no need to be
ashamed, rightly handling the word of truth. —2 Timothy 2:8-15*

*11 On the way to Jerusalem he was passing along between Samaria
and Galilee. 12 And as he entered a village, he was met by ten lepers,
who stood at a distance 13 and lifted up their voices, saying, "Jesus,
Master, have mercy on us." 14 When he saw them he said to them,
"Go and show yourselves to the priests." And as they went they were
cleansed. 15 Then one of them, when he saw that he was healed,
turned back, praising God with a loud voice; 16 and he fell on his
face at Jesus' feet, giving him thanks. Now he was a Samaritan. 17
Then Jesus answered, "Were not ten cleansed? Where are the nine?
18 Was no one found to return and give praise to God except this
foreigner?" 19 And he said to him, "Rise and go your way; your
faith has made you well." —Luke 17:11-19*

Looking back on Paul's advice to Timothy, Paul said that he was a prisoner, a Roman prisoner. He was kind of a voluntary prisoner. He identified himself as a prisoner for the gospel. Paul was a prisoner, but God's Word was not. God's Word cannot be bound. It is free, not dependent on us or on anything in this world. Nothing can stop it!

Isaiah called attention to this in Isaiah 55:11:

> *"so shall my word be that goes out from my mouth; it shall not return to me empty, but it shall accomplish that which I purpose, and shall succeed in the thing for which I sent it."*

This is a key teaching of God's Word. God's Word will manifest itself in this world come what may. So Paul says, "if we have died with Jesus Christ, then we also live with Jesus Christ" (v. 12). This is interesting because we all want life. We all want new life, abundant life, and all that new life in Christ provides. But we are also repelled by the grossness of Christ's death on the cross. We want life. We don't want death.

Nonetheless, the true teaching of the church of Jesus Christ is that our life in Christ comes out of our death to ourselves, comes out of our spiritual death, comes out of our dying to self. And this is the beginning of our new life in Christ. But if we don't die to ourselves, then that new life in Christ is never born. Regeneration comes out of our own personal death. So we must renounce self in order to embrace Christ. Both of those things need to happen.

Paul went on: "if we endure, we will also reign with him" (v. 12b). Reigning has a lot of responsibilities attached to it. It's like an athlete or musician in training. The mastery of skill requires the discipline of practice. That exercise is the practice of the fruits of the Spirit. And as good as it sounds to be loving and joyful and all those things, it's a lot more difficult than it sounds. We are not naturally good people, not moral people. We are fallen sinners. And the exercise required to make our moral muscles grow is difficult and painful. The pain cannot be avoided; it must be endured. But when the muscles have been developed, the joy of mastery blossoms and produces fruit.

Paul also said, "if we deny him, he also will deny us" (v. 12). When you walk down the street and randomly smile at somebody, they usually smile back. But if you bark at them, they will bark back. Similarly, the Lord gives us what we give Him in a sense. If we show Him animosity, He will show us animosity. If we love and submit to Him, He will love us and will give us what is best for us. And we will come to agree that His desires for us are much better than our own desires for ourselves. He has a higher calling in mind for us than we have for ourselves. But there is an exception to this.

Paul also promised that when "we are faithless, he remains faithful" (v. 12). He does not return our faithlessness. His faithfulness to us is not dependent on our faithfulness to Him. And this is a good thing, but it can have a hard edge to it. God's enduring faithfulness means that God loves us unconditionally. Remember when you were in school, if you had a hard teacher, one who pushed you pretty hard, or a coach that pushed you harder than you wanted to go. They were usually the ones that made the biggest difference to you. They caused you to work harder than you wanted to in order to make you into more than what you thought you were. The teachers and coaches who pushed us actually helped us to do more than what we thought we could do.

The other side of God's unconditional love, His unconditional faithfulness, is that He is also faithful to His promises. He is faithful to love the obedience that we give Him, but He is also faithful to judge our disobedience. And so there is kind of a negative side to God's faithfulness because His faithfulness includes His judgment for disobedience. God's love of righteousness and justice demands that He also discipline unrighteousness as part of His covenant.

When we fail to meet God's expectations for us, God does not lower His expectations for us. Rather He continues to demand that our behavior meet His expectations. Of course, He also provides grace and mercy. Grace and mercy for those who honestly engage in those practices seriously. And so it is the demanding teacher or the demanding coach—and in this case: God—that turns out to be the one who loves us the most, the one who helps us the most, the one who provides for us what we cannot or will not provide for ourselves.

Paul wrote elsewhere that what God has begun He will complete (Philippians 1:6). How will God do this? Jesus taught His disciples to remain in Him.

> *"Abide in me, and I in you. As the branch cannot bear fruit by itself, unless it abides in the vine, neither can you, unless you abide in me. I am the vine; you are the branches. Whoever abides in me and I in him, he it is that bears much fruit, for apart from me you can do nothing." (John 15:4-5).*

What does that mean? To abide means to conform to something without objection. So if you are going to abide by the rules, then you conform to the rules and you don't object to them. In this case it means to stay connected to Jesus. He is the source of our life, the true vine, from which we grow and develop into completion. Jesus is the fountain of living water from which our lives flow. Our lives are in His life.

To abide in Christ is to stay connected to Him, to His people. He is actually the source of our life. He is actually the true vine. And from Him, we grow and develop and mature. Abiding in Christ means connecting with Him every morning, every evening, every moment of every day. It means that we don't forget him. We keep ourselves interlinked with God's life so much that others can't tell where we end and where Jesus begins. We begin manifesting the character of Jesus Christ, not perfectly of course, but more and more every day. It means that we spend time alone in God's presence, and that we actually like doing that. We choose that. We find that pleasant. So we sit at Jesus' feet and we listen to his voice in prayer. We serve Him; we obey His commands; we love Him. We follow Him, and work to make disciples, as He told us to. We give joyfully, serve others freely, and love all people.

Prayer is not something where you have to go and find a specific area or a prayer closet and find some space and maybe a little book and fold your hands and close your eyes. Prayer is simply giving your attention to God. You can do it anywhere, anytime. Prayer is having an ongoing dialogue with the Lord throughout the day. It is talking to the Lord throughout the day, confiding in Him, and listening to Him

When we give thanks and praise to Jesus Christ our lives then become an act of worship. Worship is not just something that happens during an hour on Sunday morning. It is that, but it's not just that. Worship is what we do with our lives. So we practice worship in church on Sunday mornings so that when we go out into the world where the rubber meets the road, we can have muscle memory about how to live the way that Christ wants us to live. And so we practice that here in the church. We practice serving Him. We practice obeying His commands. We practice lifting up His character. We practice praying to Him. We practice loving Him. And we follow Him and His work. And we try to make disciples, first of all of ourselves, and then of others.

And as we go about trying to make disciples of others, the best way to do that is not to try to force it on people. Christianity doesn't work that way. It cannot be forced; it cannot be imposed. So we should live our lives in such a way that people notice that there is something different about us. And when they ask, *What is it about you that makes you different from other people?* When they ask that question, then you have the opportunity to answer it. But until they ask that question, they are not even thinking about it.

Christian evangelists are forever answering questions that people are not asking. So if you give people the answer before they ask the question, it won't mean anything to them. It takes time and effort to enter into long-term relationships with people that provide them with the opportunity to ask such a question, and for us to earn their trust to provide an answer that they will actually listen to.

The Lectionary turns us to Luke 17, where Jesus is on the way to Jerusalem. But, if we go back to Luke chapter 9, we find this verse that sets up the story in chapter 17:

> *"When the days drew near for him to be taken up, he set his face to go to Jerusalem" (Luke 9:51).*

It was not just that Jesus was "on the way to Jerusalem" (Luke 17:11), but that Jesus always ministered informally on the way to wherever He was going. Ministry was not a special activity, it was an ordinary activity that He did in the midst of ordinary life. This is an important detail.

But we also see that He was determined to go to Jerusalem, despite the impending danger, of which He most assuredly was aware. He would be murdered in Jerusalem—and He knew it. Yet, His earthly ministry had about six months left, and He was determined to complete His Father's business in teaching, preaching, and healing before He died.

So on His way to Jerusalem, He saw ten lepers at a distance. And it's interesting that they were at a distance because at the time people thought that leprosy was spread by contact. So lepers had no contact with people. They were shunned people. They lived outside of society. They were unable to integrate into the larger society, and they were forbidden entry into the temple.

There were ten of them, and they called out to Jesus and asked him for his mercy, which He promptly granted, and apparently healed them all. They then recognized that Jesus was Lord and Master. But they never really asked for healing, they asked for mercy. So there is an implied sense that they were asking for healing. Healing is an act of mercy.

When He saw them, He said, *go and show yourselves to the priest.* And as they went, they were cleansed. When did the healing take place? It's an interesting issue. When he saw them, he said, *go.* And they went. He gave them a command and they obeyed it. So it seems to me that the healing was in their recognition of His authority to heal. They recognized Jesus as Lord and Savior. And Jesus recognized them to be faithful because they went. Their faithfulness then trumped their leprosy. Their faith was more important than their disease. Too often we think that we are bound by our diseases. We say, *I have this or that disease. And so I can't do this or that activity.* Well, maybe you can't, and maybe you can if you just try.

But we then learn that only one was thankful. Only one turned to give thanks. And that's interesting, that's the point of the story.

Thankfulness is the essential attitude that Christians are to have. We are to be a thankful people. In fact, in Greek that word translated *thankful* is εὐχαριστία (eucharist). It is composed of two words. Eὐ means good or beneficial, and χαριστία (charis, or charity) means grace. It's an attitude. It's gratefulness. It's a beneficial thing. We are to imitate God's grace to us by giving that same grace to other people.

Nothing can keep a person from being faithful. That's the message here! Paul was not bound by Rome because God's Word cannot be bound. Paul's faith could not be bound by Rome or anything else. And neither can ours. The point is that nothing can keep a person from being faithful, grateful. Your diseases, your aches and pains, your difficulties and frustrations are a pain, but they can't keep you from being faithful.

In this story the thankful one was a Samaritan, an outcast of the worst sort. This was the one who proved to be faithful. The other nine were also healed, but they did not express their gratitude to Jesus. Does that mean that they were not saved? Maybe, but not necessarily.

There is a doctrine called Prevenient Grace. That's the grace that goes before. When we finally confront Jesus or make a decision for Christ, we find that God has been working with us, in us, before that moment. But we weren't aware of it. That's Prevenient Grace. We weren't aware that God was working in our lives before we were aware of it. But He was!

Let's assume that God healed the other nine lepers, and that their healing planted a seed in them, a prevenient grace seed. So they didn't come to Christ at that moment, but that doesn't mean that they didn't come to Christ sometime in their lives. We don't know because the story doesn't say. So as Christians, we need to err on the side of grace and mercy, and hope for the best for people.

> *"And I am sure of this, that he who began a good work in you will bring it to completion at the day of Jesus Christ" (Philippians 1:6).*

Salvation is a process. It has a beginning. It has a middle. It has an end. Salvation is a kind of waking up. And some people wake up, a bit groggy for a while. Some people wake up angry or they get up on the wrong side of the bed. And some people just pop up and they're just ready to go. People are different. But the point is that God healed the ungrateful so that in time they would become grateful, later. God is like that. He gives grace when we don't deserve the gift. If God only healed grateful people, he would have very few to heal because usually we only get grateful after the healing. He comes to us unbidden, often unwanted. He inserts Himself into our lives, demands our faithfulness, our response, our discipline, like a hard-nosed coach or teacher.

Note also that the lepers had an active role in their healing. Jesus said, "show yourselves to the Priests" (v. 14). The Priests were the gatekeepers who approved or disapproved of people being in the Temple. Did they show themselves to the Priests? Maybe, maybe not. Scripture doesn't say. Nonetheless, the point that the story makes is that few people are faithful. Paul was just repeating what Jesus said: "many are called, but few are chosen" (Matthew 22:14).

People tend to think that, if only they could see or experience a miracle, then they would believe. If God would just come down and touch them, manifest Himself at the foot of my bed and tell me some stuff, then I would believe. But that's not the reality. Nine out of ten of those lepers who were healed were ungrateful, unfaithful in the face of their healing.

Remember the story of Lazarus and the rich man. Jesus said, *if they do not listen to Moses and the prophets, they will not be convinced even if someone rises from the dead.* So people think that they need a miracle in order to believe. And we do need a miracle. But the miracle is not what we think. The miracle is regeneration. The miracle is our agreement with God, that he is Lord and Master. The miracle is the Holy Spirit who comes into us and changes our lives, changes our thinking. And so Jesus said to this ex-leper, this one who was grateful, he said, *rise and go your way. Your faith has made you well.*

The healing in this particular case wasn't a laying on of hands. It wasn't anything that we can identify. Jesus healed them as they went. He told him to go his way. The miracle happened in the ordinary flow of life. There was nothing spectacular about it. We just need to go about our lives trusting Jesus. That is the practice that will make us well. Ordinary life in Christ is, in fact, the goal of Christianity. In 1 Thessalonians 4.11 Paul says,

> *"aspire to live quietly and to mind your own affairs and to work with your hands as we instructed you".*

In other words, just be ordinary people who love Christ. That's the highest calling of the Christian community. If we're all called to be great people we will fail. The truth is that hardly any of us are going to be great. The call to be great does not resonate with most people. Only a very few will be great at anything. But we can all be ordinary, not common or average, but ordinary people who love Jesus Christ. So Paul told Timothy,

> *"to pray that we may live peaceful and quiet lives in all godliness and holiness. This is good and pleases God our Savior, who wants all people to be saved and come to the knowledge of truth" (1 Timothy 2:2-4).*

Our godly behavior directly affects our testimony and our ability to witness to other people in the world, to effectively lead people to Christ. So the exercise of faith is itself the means of our healing. It is itself the means of our wholeness and our holiness, our happiness, and our salvation. God says, *simply be faithful.* Nothing more, nothing less.

Heavenly Father, we are so privileged to know you. So privileged that you have inserted yourself into our lives, for most of us decades ago. But in spite of that, we continue to grow in fits and starts. We have our ups and we have our downs. But we pray that you would fulfill your promises and continue to call us, and draw us into your kingdom, to manifest in us the fruits of the Spirit so that we may be emissaries of Jesus Christ in this sin-torn world.

We do pray that simple faithfulness would become common, that it would be ordinary, that people would just assume it, that they would just take on Christ, that they would assume that this is just the way people are, because this is the way that you want people to be. Make it so, Father.

Continue to dispatch your Holy Spirit. Reach out, touch those who don't know you, touch those who have had a taste, but have not continued in their journey with you. We pray that you would take those who have denounced you, like the Apostle Paul before his conversion, and turn them around. Only you can do that. We can't do that for one another, but you can do that, Father. We pray that you would make it so.

We pray again for this sin-soaked, war-torn world. I fear that the drums of war are beating again, and I pray that you would silence them. We pray against war, and yet we know that it sometimes happens. So we pray for all of those who are involved in it, the perpetrators and the victims. Help us to see a better way, to see that ordinary faithfulness of people will keep us from these difficulties.

Help our leaders to know that. Cleanse them, change their hearts and minds to conform them to your son Jesus Christ. And we pray, Lord, that you would accomplish your purposes in this world, and we know that you will make restitution between yourself and all of your people, and help us to make restitution with one another. Help us to live quiet, faithful, redeemed, loving lives. In Jesus' precious name, amen.

November 9, 2022

Changes

"For behold, I create new heavens and a new earth, and the former things shall not be remembered or come into mind. 1But be glad and rejoice forever in that which I create; for behold, I create Jerusalem to be a joy, and her people to be a gladness. 19 I will rejoice in Jerusalem and be glad in my people; no more shall be heard in it the sound of weeping and the cry of distress. 20 No more shall there be in it an infant who lives but a few days, or an old man who does not fill out his days, for the young man shall die a hundred years old, and the sinner a hundred years old shall be accursed. 21 They shall build houses and inhabit them; they shall plant vineyards and eat their fruit. 22 They shall not build and another inhabit; they shall not plant and another eat; for like the days of a tree shall the days of my people be, and my chosen shall long enjoy the work of their hands. 23 They shall not labor in vain or bear children for calamity, for they shall be the offspring of the blessed of the Lord, and their descendants with them. 24 Before they call I will answer; while they are yet speaking I will hear. 25 The wolf and the lamb shall graze together; the lion shall eat straw like the ox, and dust shall be the serpent's food. They shall not hurt or destroy in all my holy mountain," says the Lord. —*Isaiah 65:17-25*

5 And while some were speaking of the temple, how it was adorned with noble stones and offerings, he said, 6 "As for these things that you see, the days will come when there will not be left here one stone upon another that will not be thrown down." 7 And they asked him, "Teacher, when will these things be, and what will be the sign when these things are about to take place?" 8 And he said, "See that you

are not led astray. For many will come in my name, saying, 'I am he!'
and, 'The time is at hand!' Do not go after them. 9 And when you
hear of wars and tumults, do not be terrified, for these things must first
take place, but the end will not be at once."10 Then he said to them,
"Nation will rise against nation, and kingdom against kingdom. 11
There will be great earthquakes, and in various places famines and
pestilences. And there will be terrors and great signs from heaven. 12
But before all this they will lay their hands on you and persecute you,
delivering you up to the synagogues and prisons, and you will be
brought before kings and governors for my name's sake. 13 This will
be your opportunity to bear witness. 14 Settle it therefore in your
minds not to meditate beforehand how to answer, 15 for I will give
you a mouth and wisdom, which none of your adversaries will be able
to withstand or contradict. 16 You will be delivered up even by parents
and brothers and relatives and friends, and some of you they will put
to death. 17 You will be hated by all for my name's sake. 18 But not
a hair of your head will perish. 19 By your endurance you will gain
your lives.

—Luke 21:5-19

Again, this is not scripture that I would have chosen. The lectionary has given it, so we need to deal with it. The lectionary is focusing on the season of the darkness of the world before the birth of Christ. Christmas is coming, but it comes at the darkest hour. God's judgment is about making changes in the world. To understand this means that we first must understand what judgment is. The dictionary tells us that it is: 1) The act or process of judging; the formation of an opinion after consideration or deliberation. Another word for it is evaluation. God is making an evaluation of things. 2) An opinion or estimate formed after consideration or deliberation, especially a formal or authoritative decision. 3) The mental ability to perceive and distinguish relationships; discernment.

We make determinations about various things all the time. It's actually impossible to go through life without making judgments, without making evaluations. Usually when we think of the word *judgment*, especially in church, we tend to think of God as the great judge who will render a verdict of guilty or innocent to His people. All of that is true, and God's verdict regarding the guilt or innocence of mankind is guilty. Right? We're all sinners. We're all guilty of disobedience to God's law. And we know that, so we have a tendency to think of judgment as a negative thing. This is pretty much the story of the Old Testament.

Over and over again, judgment comes and the world is evaluated on God's terms, and it's not so good. He brings correction that causes issues and difficulties, nations rise and nations fall. However, the Old Testament does not leave the story there. The Old Testament always looks to the future to a time when God would provide a Savior who would make things different. In the midst of Old Testament judgment, there was much hope. In the midst of the Old Testament judgments, there was always hope planted at the end of God's judgments, the hope of Christ to come.

The New Testament is the story of that Savior, Jesus Christ, who came to earth when the earth was covered in the darkness of sin. However, Jesus Christ has not made humanity, individually or collectively, innocent. Innocent people don't need forgiveness; guilty people need forgiveness. Jesus did not change the judgment of God. We are still guilty. Christians are forgiven, not innocent. But our forgiveness hinges on a condition: we must actually love God. We must love the God who condemns us! This is the great stumbling block that people trip over.

How can we love the One who condemns us? Only by the power and presence of the Holy Spirit through regeneration. We are given a new heart, a new perspective on life. In Christ, we see things from God's perspective, not just our own. In Christ, then, we come to see the purpose of God's law. We come to see that God's law or God's way is established for our good, for our flourishing. It is given to provide maximum freedom and maximum happiness in this world. God's law is for our well-being.

But prior to this new heart, we don't see any of this. We think that *we* know what is best for us. So we reject God's law because we think that it limits our freedom to pursue our happiness. We are self-focused and self-concerned, not realizing that our selfishness is the problem. When everyone is self-focused, our interests and pursuits end up in conflict, which produces strife, disharmony, and war. We become antagonistic to one another and to God.

This was the character of the people that Isaiah addressed. God had given Israel everything: escape from slavery, freedom, the law, the temple, the culture, and the opportunity to engage God by protecting them from the godless people and cultures of the world. God got His people out of Egypt, but getting Egypt out of His people proved to be more difficult. God knew this would happen, but we—humanity—needed to understand the problem from God's perspective.

So in Isaiah 65 we see God's promise to "create new heavens and a new earth" (v. 17). Isaiah wrote in the 700s B.C. That's 2700 years ago. It is important to understand that Isaiah was not writing to us who live in 2022 A.D. There is much we can learn from Isaiah, and Isaiah's work has serious application to us. Of course, God had us in mind, as He always has all of His people in mind. But Isaiah did not.

The change that Isaiah was promising came through Jesus, who was born 700 years after Isaiah wrote. That's the context of this verse. To ignore or deny this is an error. Isaiah was giving people hope that God was going to bring a change, a great change to the world. Don't neglect that God had already given Israel everything that they needed. Again, God had taken them out of slavery in Egypt. He brought them freedom. He gave them the law which was an opportunity for maximum freedom and happiness. He gave them the temple. He gave them the culture that they needed. He gave them the opportunity to engage God by protecting them from the godless people and cultures around them. He took them out into the desert where they could be isolated from the world's sin.

But in spite of all of this the new world that Isaiah envisioned only developed as the result of the life, ministry, and death of Jesus Christ. The world that developed after Jesus Christ was radically different from the world before He was born. We need to keep this context in mind. The world that Jesus came into was different from the world in Isaiah's day. And the world keeps changing.

Has the world changed since the birth of Christ? Absolutely! The changes are absolutely phenomenal. The world that developed after

Jesus Christ was in fact radically different from the world that was before Jesus Christ. We need to keep this context in mind also. Science and technology developed in the wake of Christianity because Christianity provided a true understanding of the world, and encouraged integrity, industry, and biblical morality among people.

Of course, the complete fulfillment of Isaiah's vision has still not yet happened. And that's the ongoing story of human history. God is not finished with us yet.

In many ways He's barely gotten started. And yet our world in 2022 is radically different than even the world Jesus knew! Everything is very different. We've come a long way, but we have a much longer way to go. God is still in the business of changing hearts and minds.

In Luke 21 Jesus continued the vision of Isaiah. Isaiah had written long before the Babylonian captivity. Isaiah was writing about the condition of the first Temple, which was destroyed in 722 B.C. Things were bad then. Later, Jeremiah wrote about the Temple that was destroyed again in 586 B.C. That's 250 years later, and things were still bad. Jesus was preaching 600 years after Jeremiah, and things were still bad.

Over the centuries Israel had institutionalized her rebelliousness in the name of God! And this is what Jesus was preaching against. It had been going on for a very long time. Jesus was saying that the Temple rot would require a complete rebuild. God's original plans for the Temple were good, but the execution of those plans by the Jews had been a complete failure. God had sent many prophets to straighten things out, but they were rejected by the establishment, the leaders. In order to do a complete rebuild, God would need to, not just gut the building—He'd done that a couple of times before to no avail. So He'd need to lay a new foundation and start over. And to lay a new foundation, the old building would have to be leveled.

For the Jews, it was the end of the world, and it would be the end of their place among the nations of the world. Rome burned Jerusalem and destroyed the Temple in A.D. 70. The Jewish wars began in A.D. 66 as a Jewish revolt against Rome's authority. Titus and his Roman legions arrived at Jerusalem during passover of A.D. 70. The Romans built embankments of earthen works, built battering rams, and the siege began.

The Roman army numbered 30,000; the Jewish army numbered 24,000. According to Tactitus there were 600,000 visitors crowding the streets of Jerusalem for the Passover. After five months the Temple was burned, and the walls of Jerusalem were destroyed, all except Herod's three great towers at the northwest corner of the city. Over a million people had been killed, a hundred thousand captives were taken as prisoners, among them was Josephus, an historian who wrote about it. It was the largest catastrophe in human history to date.

This was the event, the destruction, that Jesus predicted, and which happened just forty years after His death. The failure to learn about and understand this has led to much prophetic confusion in the history of Christianity. This disaster was the fulfillment of many biblical predictions about God's judgment. But the fulfillment of biblical predictions does not mean that God is finished with us. Not at all! Rather, the fulfillment of biblical predictions shows us how God's judgment works. God's plan for, not just the survival, but the flourishing of, humanity, is well documented. God has provided His law, and sent Jesus Christ to provide a proper understanding of His law, and also sent the Holy Spirit to inhabit the hearts and minds of His people to give them the desire to be faithful.

He has done all of this as an act of free grace because our history has shown that we cannot and will not listen of our own accord. So Jesus sent the Holy Spirit because God's Holy Spirit causes us to listen. And when we listen, things go well. But when we don't listen, things don't go well. So we can judge our listening skills by how things are going. When things are not going well we need to improve our listening skills. God has given us ears to hear; now we need to listen.

Heavenly Father, we are so blessed, blessed above all of the peoples of the world. We are blessed to have your Spirit in our lives personally, corporately, and as a church. We are blessed to know you. We are blessed that you have inserted yourself into our lives. And we give you thanks and praise for that.

We now pray that you would pour out your Holy Spirit upon all of your people across the face of this globe. We are in need of renewal and revival. And I'd like to be excited about that. But from your perspective, Father, I'm sure you are saying, *Oi vey! You need revival again?* We keep going through this boom and bust of revival and relapse. Help us, Father, to exit that pattern and to simply be faithful.

In the midst of our election season, we get convinced that what we need to do is we need to elect good leaders. And I'm not saying we shouldn't elect good leaders. But we've been trying to elect good leaders for an awful long time. And it doesn't seem to have changed much.

When I look around the world and try to evaluate it, make some judgments or evaluations of my own from your perspective, it looks to me like what we need is simple ordinary faith, common, ordinary faithfulness among your people. So help us to do that. We can't do that for anybody else. We can only do that for ourselves. So help us to do that.

Help us to imitate you like Paul was imitating you or to imitate Paul like the apostles were imitating Paul. Help us to be the people that you have called us to be. Give us the wisdom to see the simplicity of faithfulness and the courage to believe that by being faithful things will work out for the better, for those who love you.

We also pray for the world that is lost in sin. We pray not only for our leaders, but we pray for all of the followers of the world. Poor out your spirit, Father. Open hearts and minds to see your gospel, your truth, your Bible, your people, as you see them: sinners, guilty, forgiven, saved.

Help us Father, strengthen us, provide for us the things that only you can provide. Give us strength and courage to be who you've called us to be. The Lord has given us everything that we need. He has poured His spirit into us. I pray that you will take advantage of that. We offer ourselves to your service in Jesus' name. Amen.

November 13, 2022

The Seed

11 being strengthened with all power, according to his glorious might, for all endurance and patience with joy; 12 giving thanks to the Father, who has qualified you to share in the inheritance of the saints in light. 13 He has delivered us from the domain of darkness and transferred us to the kingdom of his beloved Son, 14 in whom we have redemption, the forgiveness of sins. 15 He is the image of the invisible God, the firstborn of all creation. 16 For by him all things were created, in heaven and on earth, visible and invisible, whether thrones or dominions or rulers or authorities—all things were created through him and for him. 17 And he is before all things, and in him all things hold together. 18 And he is the head of the body, the church. He is the beginning, the firstborn from the dead, that in everything he might be preeminent. 19 For in him all the fullness of God was pleased to dwell, 20 and through him to reconcile to himself all things, whether on earth or in heaven, making peace by the blood of his cross.

—Colossians 1:11-20

33 And when they came to the place that is called The Skull, there they crucified him, and the criminals, one on his right and one on his left. 34 And Jesus said, "Father, forgive them, for they know not what they do." And they cast lots to divide his garments. 35 And the people stood by, watching, but the rulers scoffed at him, saying, "He saved others; let him save himself, if he is the Christ of God, his Chosen One!" 36 The soldiers also mocked him, coming up and offering him sour wine 37 and saying, "If you are the King of the Jews, save yourself!" 38 There was also an inscription over him, "This is the King of the Jews."39 One of the criminals who were hanged railed at him, saying, "Are you not the Christ? Save yourself and us!" 40 But the other rebuked him, saying, "Do you not fear God, since you are under the same sentence of condemnation? 41 And we indeed justly, for we are receiving the due reward of our deeds; but this man has done nothing wrong." 42 And he said, "Jesus, remember me when you come into your kingdom." 43 And he said to him, "Truly, I say to you, today you will be with me in paradise." —*Luke 23:33-43*

What is a seed? Seeds propagate. They transmit the same characteristics from one generation to another. Seeds grow and reproduce more seeds, more of the same over time. Jesus Christ is the seed of a new humanity, a new way of being human in the world. In the Garden Adam was a *homo sapien*. The word *homo* means human being, and *sapien* comes from *sapience*, which means wisdom. *Homo sapien* is the merger of humanity and wisdom. Or you might think of it as language developing among human beings, because with Adam history begins, language began to be written down.

The new seed of Christ is *homo Christos*. Christ represents a new creation, a new kind of being in the world. This new type of human being is superior to the model of Adam, superior to the model of *homo sapien*. Christ is *homo Christos,* Christ fused to flesh. Here's what Peter had to say about this.

"Having purified your souls by your obedience to the truth for a sincere brotherly love, love one another earnestly from a pure heart, 23 since you have been born again, not of perishable seed but of imperishable, through the living and abiding word of God" (1 Peter 1:22-23)

The church is not only the body of Christ, we are the seeds of Christ. According to Colossians 1:11, God has given us "all power, according to his glorious might, for all endurance and patience." This means that we are able to be what God has made us to be in Christ. We are able to be part of God's new creation. God has not given us an impossible task. It is possible.

In addition "he has qualified" (Colossians 1:11) us. God doesn't call the qualified, He qualifies the called. None of us are qualified in ourselves to be what God has called us to be, none of us are able in our own abilities and strengths to be what God has called us to be or to do what God has called us to do. Yet all of us are able to be what God has called us to be because He has given us His Holy Spirit to make it so. God qualifies us to do that as we step up to the plate. If we don't step up to the plate, then God doesn't engage us. But when we step up to the plate, God engages us with His Holy Spirit. He has given us His Holy Spirit in order to make it so because we couldn't make it so on our own. There's no way in our own strength that we can be what God calls us to be.

All Christians "share in the inheritance of the saints in light" (1 Colossians 1:12). We are not in it alone. We are in it together. God has called us together in Christ to be the hands and feet of Christ for the world. Not perfectly, not all at once, but little by little, day by day, in our ordinary lives, as His church.

He "has delivered us from the domain of darkness and transferred us to the kingdom of his beloved Son" (1 Colossians 1:14). We are not who we used to be. We are not defined by our past. We are defined by God's future. We are becoming who God has called us to be in Christ. Not by ourselves, but together in Christ we lean into God's future. We are becoming what God ultimately is going to make us. That's who we actually are now, though like children we are not yet all that we will become. We are not who *we* think we are. We are who *God* has made us to be.

Having one foot in the kingdom, we are in the kingdom already, not entirely, but sufficiently. We like to say that we are going to heaven, and that's true. But we are already in Christ. We have already begun in Christ. And when we get there, heaven will be here. God's plan is "on earth as it is heaven." We pray for this every week. God has planted His seed, Jesus Christ, on earth. And that Seed is transmitting the same characteristics (Christ's characteristics) from one generation to another. Seeds grow and reproduce more seeds, more of the same kind.

God has redeemed us, is redeeming us through the forgiveness of sins (Colossians 1:14). To redeem is to recover ownership, to convert, to fulfill, to reinstate. God's method of redemption is through the forgiveness of sins. He is redeeming us. What does redeem mean? Most of you are old enough to remember Green Stamps. We used to save them and then redeem them at the Green Stamp store. What does that mean? You trade in your collection of stamps for something of greater value. And that is exactly what is happening with Jesus Christ.

But it's odd because when we look at the world, when we look at our lives, it doesn't seem like all this stuff is happening. It may be hard to look at our world and see that God is in the process of redeeming it, but He is. And so God calls us then to engage that process with joy and thanksgiving.

What is joy? A number of years ago, it struck me that I wasn't quite sure what joy was. So in my usual matter, I turned to the dictionary. And I learned the difference between joy and happiness. Happiness is exaltation *because* of our circumstances. So if you get good circumstances, you win the lottery or whatever and you're happy, you're exalting. Things are really great because of your circumstances. That's what happiness is.

But joy is exaltation *in spite of* our circumstances. Regardless of what is going on in your life, joy is what we are called to express, what we are called to be and to do. We are called to be joyful. Of course, we all want to be happy. Happiness is in our national constitution. But God calls us to joy, and joy is a discipline. Joy takes practice, like medicine or music. It's an art. It's like a musical skill. It takes practice to master it. It's hard to be joyful when circumstances aren't very good. But that is exactly what God is calling us to.

And so as we practice and as we study God's Word, over time, our practice and our study become fulfilling, become amazingly satisfying. And pretty soon, joy begins to bubble up and to spill over into everything. Over time our joy becomes more than what we could ever have imagined it to be.

Christ is the image of God made visible. And as we study and practice the characteristics of Jesus Christ—love, joy, peace, patience, kindness, goodness, faithfulness, gentleness, self-control; we also need to think of 1 Corinthians 13, the love chapter.

> *"Love does not envy, it does not boast, it is not proud. 5 It does not dishonor others, it is not self-seeking, it is not easily angered, it keeps no record of wrongs. 6 Love does not delight in evil but rejoices with the truth. 7 It always protects, always trusts, always hopes, always perseveres" (1 Corinthians 13:4-7).*

These are the characteristics of God that He is reproducing in His seeds. As we do these things in our own lives the image of God is made more visible in the world. This is the image of God made visible. And we, then, as seeds of Christ, are the image of God made more visible in the world. This is our calling.

Christ is the "firstborn of the dead" (Colossians 1:18). Christ is the seed of a new humanity, a new way of being human in the world. We are not there yet, but we are well on our way. Yet, much of the time, it doesn't seem that way. Why not?

Because Christ is making peace by the blood of the cross (Colossians 1:20). The blood of the cross! In the church calendar we are in the dark season, before the birth of Christ, the birth of light. Advent is the darkest season. And so the lectionary turns us to the crucifixion of Christ, which is in the darkness of human history, if you will. Israel had not heard a prophet or the Lord speak for four hundred years. The Temple had been compromised for some time. Rome dominated Jerusalem.

The crucifixion of Christ is the darkest hour in human history. It is the hour that Christ, the Seed, was put in the ground. Yes, Jesus actually died. But his death produced the germination of the Christ seed. He is reborn. And the Seed then reproduces more seeds. That's the way seeds work.

I have a giant elm tree in my backyard. It is the result of one elm seed planted in 1911. And every year it produces a gazillion elm seeds. God's method of growth is not efficiency, it's abundance and redundancy. Not every seed germinates, but seeds are also food for birds and bugs. Every seed is used. Every seed contributes to God's abundance and diversity of life. And so it is with Christ, and with us, with His church.

But here's the thing: the seed germinates in the ground, in the dark. At the darkest hour God plants His Seed. And so it is with us in the church. We are God's seed and God is using every one of us in multiple different ways. Often we don't even understand or know how God is using us, but He is. The germination of the seed happens while it's in the ground, while it's in the dark. At the darkest hour of the life of that seed is when it germinates and begins to grow. God's method is to plant His seed, to grow His seed, to germinate His seed in the darkest hours. And so we often don't see it, but we can trust that it's there, that it is growing.

When the seed goes into the ground, does the seed die? It's an interesting question. It's kind of yes and no. The seed that is planted is no more. It becomes something else. It becomes the elm tree or whatever it is that was planted. But what really happened to it? Well over time, that particular seed has become a gazillion other seeds. The seed holds the pattern, the DNA of whatever it is. And the pattern replicates. It doesn't die. The pattern lives on.

Of course, some seeds fall on the good soil and yield a crop, some a hundred fold, some sixty, some thirty. But the first Seed, the Christ Seed yields a gazillion fold over time. The Seed produces more of the same, biologically and spiritually, over time.

Time is the variable. God's time is not like our time. God's time is macrotime, our time is microtime. We're focusing on what happens tomorrow. God is focusing on what happens in a thousand years. God is very much aware of our microtime issues, and He is involved in them. But the point is that we are not aware of God's macrotime. We're not thinking a thousand years ahead, nor a hundred, not even ten. God understands our time, but we don't understand His time.

So, when we find ourselves in the darkness, we need to remember the light, for the darkness will be but a moment, but the light—an eternity! And herein lies our joy. In spite of our present circumstances, in spite of the darkness—and maybe even because of it!—God's seeds continues to grow. Just because you and I don't see the growth, doesn't mean that it isn't happening out of our sight. In fact, we can be sure that it is happening.

Jesus continued to manifest Godliness on the cross, as He was nailed and hung in agony. We read the story. They divided His garments, scoffed at Him, taunted Him, and dared Him to save Himself. But the Seed didn't need to be saved. His planting, His death, is the saving of the world. Up from the grave He arose!

At the darkest hour Jesus was crucified between two thieves.

> *"One of the criminals who were hanged railed at him, saying, 'Are you not the Christ? Save yourself and us!' But the other rebuked him, saying, 'Do you not fear God, since you are under the same sentence of condemnation? And we indeed justly, for we are receiving the due reward of our deeds; but this man has done nothing wrong.' And he said, 'Jesus, remember me when you come into your kingdom.' And he said to him, 'Truly, I say to you, today you will be with me in paradise'" (Luke 23:39-43).*

The thief who recognized Jesus as the Christ was saved in the moment of his recognition. And that's the way it works. We are saved the moment we recognize Jesus as the Christ, the savior of humanity. Everyone who is saved is saved in that moment of personal recognition. That's the point of that story. The point is not that we can wait until the last moment to be saved. We cannot put it off until the last moment. Jesus Christ is not an insurance plan that kicks in when we need it.

The thief on the cross is not the norm, he's the exception. So, it is wrong to make his salvation the norm. If you think that the point of the story is that we can wait until our deathbed to give ourselves to Christ, you're mistaken. Of course, deathbed conversions are possible, but they are not the norm. We cannot depend on them. The point of the salvation of the thief on the cross is that anyone can be saved, regardless of their past. God's people are not defined by their past. We are defined by God's future.

People are saved the moment they genuinely recognize Christ. And they can be anywhere. It doesn't have to be at church, or at a revival—anywhere. At home, at the office, in your car. On a cross. And it doesn't matter who you are, or who you think you are. Because in reality you are God's. We are God's people, even in the darkness, even when it doesn't seem like it.

Salvation doesn't depend on us, it depends on God. And God is dependable.

Heavenly Father, again we are so privileged to have you in our lives. We are privileged to have you in our church, in this world. We give you thanks and praise for sending Jesus Christ to save the likes of us, to save this world that is so soaked in sin. So we pray for that world. We pray for the world in which we live. We pray for those who don't seem to know you. We pray for those who claim to know you, but don't really follow you. We pray for those who know you and love you and are doing everything they can to follow you to the best of their ability. We are all in need of your help, Father.

Fortunately you provide that help through the power and presence of your Holy Spirit. So be with us. If you haven't germinated that seed, germinate it. Help it to grow. Help us to help it to grow. Be with our little church here. Help us to be faithful. Help us to lift up faithfulness, common, ordinary, run-of-the-mill faithfulness of ordinary people. As we look at the world it seems that that is the thing that is lacking. Sure, great leadership would be fine, but we've sent a lot of great leaders to Washington. And it doesn't seem to help. So what we need, Father, is ordinary, common faithfulness.

And the only way we can move that forward is by engaging it ourselves and sharing it with others when it's appropriate and when we are able. So help us to do that. Help all of your people to do that. Help all of your seeds to grow, to manifest your character in their lives, in our lives, in our church, in our communities, at our workplaces. Help us to be the people that you've called us to be, in Jesus' name. Amen.

November 20, 2022

THE MIRTH OF CHRIST: TODAY

"10 Love does no wrong to a neighbor; therefore love is the fulfilling of the law. 11 Besides this you know the time, that the hour has come for you to wake from sleep. For salvation is nearer to us now than when we first believed. 12 The night is far gone; the day is at hand. So then let us cast off the works of darkness and put on the armor of light. 13 Let us walk properly as in the daytime, not in orgies and drunkenness, not in sexual immorality and sensuality, not in quarreling and jealousy. 14 But put on the Lord Jesus Christ, and make no provision for the flesh, to gratify its desires."

—Romans 13:10-14

36 "But concerning that day and hour no one knows, not even the angels of heaven, nor the Son, but the Father only. 37 For as were the days of Noah, so will be the coming of the Son of Man. 38 For as in those days before the flood they were eating and drinking, marrying and giving in marriage, until the day when Noah entered the ark, 39 and they were unaware until the flood came and swept them all away, so will be the coming of the Son of Man. 40 Then two men will be in the field; one will be taken and one left. 41 Two women will be grinding at the mill; one will be taken and one left. 42 Therefore, stay awake, for you do not know on what day your Lord is coming. 43 But know this, that if the master of the house had known in what part of the night the thief was coming, he would have stayed awake and would not have let his house be broken into. 44 Therefore you also must be ready, for the Son of Man is coming at an hour you do not expect."

—Matthew 24:36-44

The hour has come," Paul said in Romans 13. By the time Paul had written Romans, he was well into his ministry. Jesus had come and died and had returned only to be raised up at His ascension. In Romans 13 Paul was talking about how to live in the kingdom of God. The time had come for Christians to wake up from their stupor and step into the kingdom. And how were people supposed to do that? Paul left instructions: The first thing to note here is that, while Paul had spoken a lot about freedom and new life in Christ, the kind of freedom that Paul preached was not the abandonment of God's law.

> *"Love does no wrong to a neighbor; therefore love is the fulfilling of the law," he said in v. 10.*

Rather than dispensing with God's law, Paul said that love, real love, Christian love, agape love, fulfills the law. Agape love is love without expectation of any return; love without conditions; love that is not based on feelings. Agape love is the practice of always doing what is best for the other person regardless of how you feel about it. And the time to begin practicing this love is "now" said Paul.

Of course his "now" is our "back then," but his "now" is also always the ever-present now. The immediacy of "now" is always with us, which means that "now" is anytime that a person realizes it. Now is when we make it real, when we really begin practicing it. And love, like medicine, is a practice, an art. Like a musical instrument it takes time, discipline, and dedication to master. While no one masters it perfectly, we all can continue to grow and improve in our practice all our lives. We never outgrow it. We always need to keep practicing it.

Love is always a matter of sharing it, of giving it away. But we can't give what we don't have. We can't teach what we don't know. We can't share what we have not experienced. Fortunately, God has already given us agape love, love without conditions. And the Holy Spirit has given us the experience both of receiving this love from the Lord and the opportunity of sharing that love with other people.

Christ is teaching us agape love, love that is radically focused on doing what is best for the other person regardless of how we feel. And the Holy Spirit has given us the experience of both receiving and sharing agape love with others. So, now we can give what we have; we can teach what we know—even if we know very little, what we do know in Christ is good and right and wholesome. And we can share our experience with others.

Paul said, "for the hour has come" (v. 10). In this Advent/Christmas season and in every Advent/Christmas season, the hour is upon us. It is time "to wake from sleep. For salvation is nearer to us now than when we first believed" (v. 10). Not only is the meaning of Christmas related to Christ's birth, but it is also a time to celebrate the new life in Christ when someone accepts Jesus Christ as their Savior. That is also a birth of Christ event. And it is also the anticipation of Jesus returning again, the rebirth of humanity in Christ.

Christmas is about Christ, about new life in Christ, and about the fulfillment of time when Christ will return. At Christmas we celebrate the "was," the "is," and the "will be" of our Lord; the past, present, and future of Jesus Christ. And how do we do this?

> *"So then let us cast off the works of darkness and put on the armor of light" (v. 12).*

We must abandon our past, our history, and embrace Christ's future for us. Paul cataloged some of the works of darkness in Galatians 5:19-21:

> *"sexual immorality, impurity, sensuality, idolatry, sorcery, enmity, strife, jealousy, fits of anger, rivalries, dissensions, divisions, envy, drunkenness, orgies, and things like these."*

He repeated some of them in Romans 13:13:

> *"Let us walk properly as in the daytime, not in orgies and drunkenness, not in sexual immorality and sensuality, not in quarreling and jealousy."*

How do we do that? How do we "put on the Lord Jesus Christ" (v. 14). If history is our judge, not very well, because we as a society still do a bunch of the things Paul listed in Galatians 5:19-21 and/or Romans 13:13. So Paul gives us more instruction. He said, "put on the Lord Jesus Christ" (v. 14). It's kind of like a cloak or a coat. You wear it. So, why do we put on Jesus Christ? Isn't that fake? Doesn't that hide us, cover us from being seen in our nakedness? Yes, it does. But it's not any different than the clothes that we are currently wearing. They are not fake. They don't hide who we are. But they do cover our nakedness, if you will, so that people see the clothes we are wearing and not get distracted by our nakedness. So when you put on Christ, it's the same kind of thing. We wear Christ for the same reasons. It's so that people will see Christ on you, so that when you go out, they will see that you are wearing Christ, that you are presenting Christ. That's how we do it. We re-present Christ to the world.

Paul went on to say that we should not be concerned about ourselves, our flesh and desires. We should not be concerned about ourselves, our own satisfaction. Why not? Because God will take care of us. And this is a lot more than just some flowery phrase.

Agape love in a marriage provides the model. Here is how it is supposed to work: the husband puts the needs and desires of his wife above his own; and the wife puts the needs and desires of her husband above her own. Each submits to and cares for the other sacrificially, forsaking his or her own needs and desires, and serving the needs and desires of the other.

And by forsaking our own needs and desires, giving ourselves completely to the needs and desires of the other, and being in relationship with Christ and with one another, we find that all are well cared for. Again, each submits to and cares for the other, sacrificially, forsaking his or her own needs and desires in order to meet the needs and desires of the other person in the marriage. It's a great model. We don't have to worry about ourselves, rather we worry about the other, who worries about us.

In Matthew 24 Jesus was talking about the end of the Jewish Temple system, which was swept from history in A.D. 70 when Rome destroyed Jerusalem and the Temple. In v. 34 Jesus said,

"Truly, I say to you, this generation will not pass away until all these things take place. Heaven and earth will pass away, but my words will not pass away."

And, sure enough, forty years later it happened. But at the time, no one knew when it would happen, not even Jesus, who said,

"But concerning that day and hour no one knows, not even the angels of heaven, nor the Son, but the Father only" (v. 36).

It is easy to get confused about this if you don't know about the destruction of Jerusalem and the Temple in A.D. 70. A lot of people today think that Jesus was talking about something that is still in our future. But that is not what Jesus was talking about. And yet, if we understand the biblical pattern of God's faithlessness and judgment, and the promise of His faithfulness and blessing; then we can still see that there is some contemporary application of God's promise and God's curse today.

The lesson taught in this story is that faithlessness and disobedience leads to destruction. God was willing to destroy His own chosen people and His Temple in order to enforce this lesson. This should concern us very much because this pattern of history is still going on. God has blessed America, but His blessing is still subject to our faithfulness and obedience. Jesus did not change this pattern. Rather, He provided a way for us to actually be faithful without being perfect. But the story, our story, is not over. God is in the process of weighing us, weighing the world in His scales. Our day of judgment is still in the future, and only God knows the timing.

But remember that *judgment* doesn't mean destruction. It means *evaluation.* Passing God's evaluation provides a different future than failing His evaluation. For the faithful, God's judgment is a blessing; for the faithless it is not. Jesus mentioned that the coming of the Son of Man would be like Noah's story. People did not believe Noah, and disregarded his warnings. And the destruction of the flood was disastrous. It looks like Jesus was predicting that half the people of Jerusalem would parish in a catastrophe. Was He trying to scare people?

"The fear of the Lord is the beginning of wisdom, And the knowledge of the Holy One is understanding" (Proverbs 9:10).

The point of this proverb is not to be afraid, but to be prepared. What does it mean to be prepared for Christ to return? First and foremost, it means that however you need to be when He returns, in order convince Him that you love Him and are living in obedience to His commands, you need to be doing that now. If you think you can live like the devil now, and change when Christ returns, you are sorely mistaken. You are believing that the salvation of the thief on the cross was a normal pattern. It was not! And besides, that's not what the thief on the cross did. He did not postpone his response to Jesus until the last moment. His response was immediate. He only became aware of Jesus at his last moments. And as soon as he became aware he responded. That's the model, that's the pattern. Immediate response.

"Therefore you also must be ready, for the Son of Man is coming at an hour you do not expect" (v. 44).

Those who think they know when Jesus will return, or how Jesus will return, are necessarily wrong. That includes you and me. We need, not only to respond to Jesus now, we need to be ready right now and always.

This is the season we celebrate Jesus' birth: His birth thousands of years ago, His birth in our lives today, and His rebirth in the world soon. Jesus was, is, and will be—always!

Heavenly Father, again we are so grateful that you are present in our lives, present in our church, present in our community, present in this world. We give you thanks and praise for all that you have done and are doing and yet will do. And in the midst of this Christmas season, Father, help us to have an extra heap of thanksgiving. Help us to be thankful in the midst of everything. Help us to be thankful even in the midst of something like black Friday shopping.

Help us to be thankful in the midst of our stress so that we can remember Christ and we can put on Christ. Help us to remember agape love in our marriages, in our families, in our work situations everywhere. Help us to model Jesus Christ as best we can. We know that we aren't going to do it all that well. But we also know that you will bless every little effort. And we know that we do it only by the power and presence of your Holy Spirit in our lives. And we know that you will move that spirit forward to mature us as we engage that practice.

So be with us, especially during this time of Christmas. Lord, I myself have a love-hate relationship with Christmas. I love the meaning of it, and I hate what we've done with it—all of the glitz and all of the commercialism. And yet, Father, even in the midst of the glitz and the commercialism, you use this Christmas spirit to move your message forward.

In a world that doesn't know you, people open their hearts and minds at Christmas time in some ways. And you even bless this world financially in the sense that the Christmas season is, for lots of retailers, a major part of their year. And there is a blessing in that, Father. So help us to appreciate all of the aspects of Christmas.

Help us to appreciate our families and friends as we gather here and there, as best we can in the midst of all the stuff that's going on. And we pray for all of your churches, Father, all of your pastors and all of your people who gather on Sunday mornings and at other times. They all lift up the name of Jesus, and worship you in various different ways. We know we are not in agreement with them all, but we can appreciate them all. They are all trying to serve you, as we are. So we pray that you would draw all of them and all of us closer to you. Help us all to know you better, to love you more, especially during this season.

So strengthen this Father even as we pray together, in the name of Jesus Christ. Amen.

The Mirth of Christ: Expectations

*There shall come forth a shoot from the stump of Jesse, and a branch
from his roots shall bear fruit. 2 And the Spirit of the Lord shall rest
upon him, the Spirit of wisdom and understanding, the Spirit of
counsel and might, the Spirit of knowledge and the fear of the Lord.
3 And his delight shall be in the fear of the Lord. He shall not judge
by what his eyes see, or decide disputes by what his ears hear, 4 but
with righteousness he shall judge the poor, and decide with equity for
the meek of the earth; and he shall strike the earth with the rod of his
mouth, and with the breath of his lips he shall kill the wicked. 5
Righteousness shall be the belt of his waist, and faithfulness the belt
of his loins. 6 The wolf shall dwell with the lamb, and the leopard
shall lie down with the young goat, and the calf and the lion and the
fattened calf together; and a little child shall lead them. 7 The cow
and the bear shall graze; their young shall lie down together; and the
lion shall eat straw like the ox. 8 The nursing child shall play over
the hole of the cobra, and the weaned child shall put his hand on the
adder's den. 9 They shall not hurt or destroy in all my holy mountain; for the earth shall be full of the knowledge of the Lord as the
waters cover the sea. 10 In that day the root of Jesse, who shall stand
as a signal for the peoples—of him shall the nations inquire, and his
resting place shall be glorious.* —*Isaiah 11:1-10*

*4 For whatever was written in former days was written for our in-
struction, that through endurance and through the encouragement of
the Scriptures we might have hope. 5 May the God of endurance and
encouragement grant you to live in such harmony with one another,
in accord with Christ Jesus, 6 that together you may with one voice*

glorify the God and Father of our Lord Jesus Christ. 7 Therefore welcome one another as Christ has welcomed you, for the glory of God. 8 For I tell you that Christ became a servant to the circumcised to show God's truthfulness, in order to confirm the promises given to the patriarchs, 9 and in order that the Gentiles might glorify God for his mercy. As it is written, ... 12 "The root of Jesse will come, even he who arises to rule the Gentiles; in him will the Gentiles hope." 13 May the God of hope fill you with all joy and peace in believing, so that by the power of the Holy Spirit you may abound in hope.

—Romans 15:4-9, 12-13

Isaiah was predicting the Future. How was it that Isaiah could make such an accurate prediction? Well, the truth of the matter is that *he* didn't. *God* did. God showed Isaiah what the world would need, what kind of a savior He was going to send into the world. Isaiah told us about God's plan for the birth of Jesus centuries before Jesus was born.

We can't predict the weather next week. Why would God do things the way He did them? Why bother with all the waiting for the Messiah? We modern Americans hate waiting. Waiting is a waste of time. We just want what we want, and we want it now! I suppose the answer is that the world was not ready. Timing is important in gift giving. The giver has to be ready to give. The receiver has to be ready to receive. The gift has to be available. And the right method of delivery needs be engaged.

I've said this before and I'll say it again: there are different kinds of waiting. And the kind of waiting that God wants us to be engaged in, especially during this Advent period as we are waiting for Christ to come again, is not waiting *for*, but waiting *on*. The difference is like sitting at a bus stop waiting *for* a bus. That's one kind of waiting. The other kind of waiting is an active waiting, like a waiter waits *on* a table. The waiter is not just sitting around and twiddling his thumbs. A good waiter anticipates what people need and brings it to them before they ask for it. That's the kind of waiting Christians need to do in anticipation of the coming of the Lord. We need to be waiting upon the Lord, anticipating the Lord's wants and desires in our lives and in other people's lives. And then meet God's desires to the best of our ability. That's the kind of waiting that we should be engaged in.

In Isaiah 11, we see the kind of Savior that God would send to the world. The Messiah would come from the line of Jesse with the Spirit of the Lord; with wisdom, understanding, counsel, and might, full of knowledge and the fear of the Lord. The savior would need to judge with righteousness; He would need to know what is right and just. He would need to be a peacemaker, and have an abundance of self-discipline, and have all of the fruits of the Spirit.

His words would also have to bear the truth of God, which slays the wicked while maintaining faithfulness. God's Word slays wickedness by revealing its self-centeredness, like light dispels darkness. We need to distinguish between slaying the wicked and slaying wickedness because it's much more effective to get rid of wickedness. If you just get rid of wicked people, there will always be more people because people are naturally wicked and sinful. But if you eliminate wickedness itself, defeat the ideology, the problem is solved. Of course, only God can do that, and He is working on it.

> *"In that day the root of Jesse, who shall stand as a signal for the peoples—of him shall the nations inquire, and his resting place shall be glorious" (v. 10).*

We know that Isaiah was talking about Jesus, long before Jesus was born. How could he do that? Because Isaiah was talking about the character of the savior. His character is more important than His lineage, His family. Why? Because His character, the Character of the Savior, of Jesus, would one day be the norm for humanity. The new humanity in Christ, *homo Christos*, is patterned after the Character or Person of Jesus, the Character of God in human flesh.

In Christ God is manifest in the world, first through Jesus, then through those who imitate Jesus. Christians would one day be—and are now—called to emulate the Character or Person of Jesus Christ, to reproduce the fruits of the Spirit in their own lives. The thing that makes Jesus Christ the Savior of the world is His manifestation of the Character of God. He lived in the fruits of the Spirit.

Christians would one day be—and are now—called to emulate or copy the character of Jesus, to reproduce the fruits of the spirit in our own lives. The thing that makes Jesus Christ the Savior of the world is the fact that he manifested the Character of God perfectly. While we can't do that perfectly, we can do it seriously, genuinely, to the best of our flawed ability.

> *"Be imitators of me, as I am of Christ" (1 Corinthians 11:1). "For whatever was written in former days was written for our instruction, that through endurance and through the encouragement of the Scriptures we might have hope" (Romans 15:4).*

Paul said this about the Old Testament; and now we can say it about Paul, who for us, was writing in "former days." For us, Paul lived in former days.

Isaiah expected that God's savior would come one day. Isaiah hoped for it, and the Jews hoped for a Savior for seven hundred years after Isaiah wrote these words, before Jesus came. Faithful Jews refused to stop hoping; they hoped with the expectation of fulfillment. They hoped until their hope came true. That is a great model of faithfulness!

But when Jesus did finally come, they couldn't believe it! They refused to believe it. That's the story of the New Testament. Of course, that came later, long after Isaiah wrote about it. But I'm getting ahead of the story! The rejection of Jesus comes in Lent. We'll talk about that in six months or so.

The context of our Romans reading is that Paul was talking to two groups in the church who were in conflict: the strong and the weak. He was exhorting both the strong and the weak to accept one another, because they are both accepted by Christ, even though they are both sinners. Such mutual acceptance will bring great glory to God. Notice that the reason for the conflict is immaterial. We are all suppose to live "in accord with Christ Jesus" (v. 5). The Greek word (ὁμοθυμαδὸν) really means one mind or one mouth. It can be translated either way; the mind and the mouth are connected.

But here's the thing: Paul said that we should live in accord with *Christ Jesus*. But quite often we confuse ourselves by thinking that we need to live in accord with *one another*. But that's not what Paul said, not entirely. We are not to simply live in accord with each other, but each one of us is to live in accord with the glory of God in Christ Jesus. Each of us should be glorifying God. Each should be primarily striving to think and live in accord with God in the light of Jesus Christ.

This is the illusive unity of God's people that has failed to manifest in the modern world. We are not to be in agreement with one another first, but rather all of God's people are to be first in agreement with God. And because God is Trinitarian, God has various perspectives that are in accord with each other. God is a complex of three Persons: Father, Son, and Holy Spirit.

In a sense it works like this: If you've got two people who are not in agreement with one another, they need to work to be in agreement with Jesus Christ first. If they can each agree with Jesus Christ, and get in line with Jesus Christ, they will get closer together to one another in their unity with Christ. But Christ has to be the first priority for both. This is the illusive unity of God's people that is talked about and sought after.

The unity of God's people is not found in our agreement with one another, but is found in our mutual agreement with God in Christ. And because God is Trinitarian, Father, Son, and Holy Spirit, God has different perspectives. The Father sees things one way, the Son sees things another way, and the Holy Spirit sees things in still another way. And yet all these different ways are in unity or harmony in the Trinity. In the Trinity these differing ways of seeing things are in unity, agreement or harmony. The Persons of the Godhead see things from different perspectives, but those perspectives are in deep harmony with one another. They are not in disagreement.

Thus, Christian unity is not monolithic agreement about every jot and tittle of Scripture. Christian unity is not denominational agreement. Rather, Christian unity is an attitude of praise and the acceptance of praise regarding Jesus Christ. Christians are unified in their praise of God, though they express their praise differently.

"May the God of endurance and encouragement grant you to live in such harmony with one another, in accord with Christ Jesus, that together you may with one voice glorify the God and Father of our Lord Jesus Christ. Therefore welcome one another as Christ has welcomed you, for the glory of God" (Romans 15:5 -7).

The Old Testament Jews had convinced themselves that God intended to save only them, only the Jews. They had become self-concerned, self-focused, and intended to keep the gospel to themselves. But that was never what God had promised. They had not become the blessing to the nations that God charged Abraham to become. The job of the coming Messiah was to clarify this to the Jews, who did not want to hear it.

"Christ became a servant to the circumcised (the Jews) to show God's truthfulness" (v. 8). God would keep His promise to the Jews, though the Jews did not keep their promise to God. The Jews would be saved just like everyone else had always been saved, "by grace through faith." Christ also "became a servant to the circumcised (the Jews) "in order to confirm the promises given to the patriarchs." God's promise of salvation was thousands of years old, yet God intended to keep it in order to show the Jews that He (God) was faithful to His promise. Christ also "became a servant to the circumcised (the Jews) in order that the Gentiles might glorify God for his mercy." Because God's promise to save Jew and Gentile alike was thousands of years old (Genesis 12:15), even the Gentiles would see God's faithfulness and give Him glory.

So Paul quoted Isaiah's prophecy to show that in Christ that prophecy was being fulfilled. Paul was saying that the coming of Jesus Christ was the fulfillment of the highest hope, the greatest prophecy of the Old Testament, that in Christ the kingdom of God had actually come to earth. The end (the purpose for which the world had been created) had come in Jesus Christ. That's a very big claim! We can see it now, but to see it then was very difficult.

Of course, Christ's toe-hold in Jerusalem was only the beginning. The fullness of the kingdom would be millennia (thousands of years) in the coming. The Christmas message is that Christ has come, the kingdom is here, now is the time. It has already begun. It's not complete yet, but it's growing. Paul was lifting up the persistence of hope for the world in the midst of the darkness of a world devoid of Christ. And in the darkness of the Advent season (not just the shorter days, but the moral darkness of historical and contemporary faithlessness) we find the persistence of hope that Jesus Christ will see us through it all, that God will accomplish what He has begun.

> *"May the God of hope fill you with all joy (Joy, not happiness. Joy in spite of our circumstances) and peace in believing, so that by the power of the Holy Spirit you may abound in hope" (Romans 15:13).*

Hope is the life-blood of the gospel, especially hope that abounds in joy! This is the place. We are the people. The time is now.

Heavenly Father, again, we are thankful for your presence in our lives, for your presence in this world. We are thankful that you sent Jesus Christ to save the likes of us. Help us, Father, to be thankful in the midst of all things. And we thank you for this church, and pray for your continued mission through this church. Help us to be hopeful in the midst of our circumstances. Because our hope, Father, is not dependent upon us, it's dependent upon you. We are not going to bring it to bear, but you are, and we can trust that. So help us to trust you, to trust your Spirit, your Christ, in our lives.

And we do pray for this world, Father. In many ways it does seem to be dark. The drums of war are beating. We don't like much of the news that we hear. And yet the reason that we feel bad about it is because we have a glimmer of hope about how the world could be in you. If we were to all manifest your Spirit, Father, the world would be a very different place. And because we see that, and because we know that that is possible, we look at the condition of the world, and we feel bad for it. But that badness that we feel is a part of your revelation. You are revealing to us the state of the world in which we live. We recognize the evil only because of the goodness that you have dispatched to us in Christ Jesus. Apart from Christ we would not recognize the evil.

We pray that you will continue the mission of Jesus Christ who reveals to us and to the whole world the state of the world. We know that you have provided for this broken world in the fullness of your love, to help us to be who you called us to be. So we pray that you would pour out your Holy Spirit and open the eyes and the ears of many in your church and out.

Because others also see the darkness of the world, we pray that they might see a glimmer of light here and there through our activity, through our church, through all of your churches, and through your Holy Spirit. We pray that people will be attracted enough to that light to engage it, to engage you. Make it so, Father.

And we thank you for this Christmas season, though for many it is a blue Christmas. Christmas involves gatherings of family, and as those families gather, we are aware of ruptures in relationships and such that are often difficult and painful. So we pray for peace and patience and healing in the midst of all of those family gatherings.

We pray for your spirit of healing to work in us and through us in little ways, to help us to be your hands and your feet here and there as best we are able. In Jesus' name, amen.

December 11, 2022

THE MIRTH OF CHRIST: RISE UP

46 And Mary said, "My soul magnifies the Lord, 47 and my spirit rejoices in God my Savior, 48 for he has looked on the humble estate of his servant. For behold, from now on all generations will call me blessed; 49 for he who is mighty has done great things for me, and holy is his name. 50 And his mercy is for those who fear him from generation to generation. 51 He has shown strength with his arm; he has scattered the proud in the thoughts of their hearts; 52 he has brought down the mighty from their thrones and exalted those of humble estate; 53 he has filled the hungry with good things, and the rich he has sent away empty. 54 He has helped his servant Israel, in remembrance of his mercy, 55 as he spoke to our fathers, to Abraham and to his offspring forever" —*Luke 1:46-55*

2 Count it all joy, my brothers, when you meet trials of various kinds, 3 for you know that the testing of your faith produces steadfastness. 4 And let steadfastness have its full effect, that you may be perfect and complete, lacking in nothing. 5 If any of you lacks wisdom, let him ask God, who gives generously to all without reproach, and it will be given him. … 5:7 Be patient, therefore, brothers, until the coming of the Lord. See how the farmer waits for the precious fruit of the earth, being patient about it, until it receives the early and the late rains. 8 You also, be patient. Establish your hearts, for the coming of the Lord is at hand. 9 Do not grumble against one another, brothers, so that you may not be judged; behold, the Judge is standing at the door. 10 As an example of suffering and patience, brothers, take the prophets who spoke in the name of the Lord.

—*James 1:2-5; 5:7-10*

Looking back at that first scripture reading in Luke, in order to get a hold of that, we need to be aware of the Magnificat, which is Mary's poem. We need to put it in context. So I want to remind you that it occurs in Luke 1:46-55:

"My soul magnifies the Lord,
47 and my spirit rejoices in God my Savior,
48 for he has looked on the humble estate of his servant.
For behold, from now on all generations will call me blessed;
49 for he who is mighty has done great things for me,
and holy is his name.
50 And his mercy is for those who fear him
from generation to generation.
51 He has shown strength with his arm;
he has scattered the proud in the thoughts of their hearts;
52 he has brought down the mighty from their thrones
and exalted those of humble estate;
53 he has filled the hungry with good things,
and the rich he has sent away empty.
54 He has helped his servant Israel,
in remembrance of his mercy,
55 as he spoke to our fathers,
to Abraham and to his offspring forever."

Here an angel appears to Mary and explains that even though she is a virgin she's going to give birth to the Messiah. We've heard this story a zillion times in our Christian life, but it's actually a pretty weird story. Why is it important that Christ is born of a virgin?

Let me suggest something. Jesus Christ is fully human, but is also more than human. Jesus needed to be born from a human mother in order to be human. But the Father of Jesus is not Joseph, it's God, the Holy Spirit who overshadowed Mary and left her with a child. Virgin birth was something completely different from anything that had ever happened to any other human being.

Mary had great faith, but she also had a lot of questions, and some uncertainty about it all. How would her parents and Joseph, her fiancé, respond? We know from Matthew 1 that this was an issue for Joseph, who worked through it and decided to marry her anyway.

But Mary, wanting to talk to someone outside of her immediate family circle, visited her cousin Elizabeth in the Judean hill country. Luke 1:39–45 records the meeting of Mary and Elizabeth. Elizabeth, was six months pregnant with John (the Baptist) at this time. The Holy Spirit so permeated their meeting that the moment Elizabeth heard Mary's voice her unborn baby leaped or kicked in her womb. So the first person to recognize the divinity of Jesus Christ was an unborn baby, John the Baptist. That's how we interpret it today. Elizabeth then blessed Mary and Jesus.

Mary then responded to Elizabeth's blessing with what is now commonly called the Magnificat. We're used to hearing it today, but if somebody came to you, your daughter or a friend, and said, *hey, I'm a virgin and I'm pregnant*.... Well, what are you going to think? We would have trouble with that today. But if an angel came to explain it, well, maybe we would have a better understanding. Or maybe we might doubt the angel, or the angel story. Who knows?

Magnificat is Latin and it means *magnify*. The Magnificat is poetic and is sometimes sung at various services during the Advent/Christmas season. It begins, "My soul magnifies the Lord." *Soul* in Greek is ψυχή, *psuche* or *psyche*, which is the totality of the human mind, conscious and unconscious. It is defined as the mind, emotions, and will. Soul is what makes us unique, what gives us our personal identity; it is the completeness of our life or being.

When we take a close look at Mary we see the Lord. The Spirit of God shines through the life of Mary. A magnifying glass makes things look bigger. So if you look at Mary through a magnifying glass you can see the Lord.

She goes on to say, "and my spirit rejoices in God my Savior." So now we have soul and spirit. Soul is finite; it is associated with the individual. My soul is limited to me, my life, my uniqueness, my wholeness as a person. Whereas spirit is infinite. Spirit connects me to God. The Holy Spirit in me is Christ in me, but there is more to the the Holy Spirit and Christ than just me. My spirit is a piece of God given to me, but is not all of God. Mary said that her connection with God produced joy, in spite of her difficult circumstances. She was unmarried, pregnant, engaged, and she was full of joy.

The general tenner of the Magnificat is the idea that God was blessing the humble, ordinary people, not the great people. The idea is that God uses ordinary humble people, not proud, powerful people. In Christ the Spirit of God was coming to ordinary people, humble people, common people, to humanity at large. The general idea of the Magnificat is that God was coming to Mary who was a nobody in a nobody town in a nobody country in the middle of nowhere. And Mary was amazed by it.

God is opposed to hero worship. God's salvation is not for heroes to champion, but is for ordinary people to engage and celebrate. When we look closely at the heroes of the faith, we see ordinary people. Yes, some people do extraordinary things, but most, ninety-nine percent, live ordinary lives. Christianity is not hero worship of the great saints, but is the story of Christ in the lives of ordinary people. This is the message of the Magnificat.

James said,

> *"Count it all joy, my brothers, when you meet trials of various kinds, for you know that the testing of your faith produces steadfastness. And let steadfastness have its full effect, that you may be perfect and complete, lacking in nothing" (James 1:2-4).*

This is important because it is the very first thing James wrote. Why is it important? Many Christians think that once they've made a decision for Christ everything will fall into place and life will be great. But that's not what Jesus said:

> *"If they persecuted me, they will persecute you" (John 15:20-21).*

James was preparing people for real life in Christ in a world that would be offended by His teaching. When being faithful brings offense, then difficulties become a banner of faithfulness.

We can rise above daily difficulties because we know that difficulties are birth pangs of the Holy Spirit in the world. Yes, they hurt, but the pain is temporary while the joy of the Holy Spirit is eternal. No pain, no gain. Mastering any skill requires commitment, discipline, and practice, all of which are difficult, time consuming, and often distressing. Ask anyone who is trying to master any skill and they will tell you that it's hard and not much fun most of the time. Yet they do it, and do it a lot! Why? Because they love it, and it brings them satisfaction and joy. The same is true about discipleship. Spiritual joy is different than worldly joy (or happiness). What is the difference between joy and happiness? Happiness is appropriate adaptation to your circumstances. So when people are appropriately adapted to their circumstances they are happy, content. When you win the lottery you are usually happy with your circumstance. Joy is different. Joy is happiness in spite of your circumstances. Joy is transcendent. Joy doesn't depend on our circumstances, and spiritual joy is even less dependent on our circumstances. Where worldly happiness depends on our worldly circumstances, joy does not.

Usually when things are going well people are happy and when things go poorly they are not. If you lose a loved one, or during the loss of a job or loss of a home or a bankruptcy something like that, people lose their happiness. All of those kinds of things steal our happiness away. But spiritual joy depends upon God, and God is eternally present with us. There is never a loss of connection with God. God is always available, though sometimes we fall away from Him, However, He has not shut us out, we have shut Him out.

Usually when we feel this way it is the result of our failure of commitment, discipline, and practice. So returning to these things will usually reestablish our connection with God, and our joy. The joy of the Lord is eternal, ever present, always available. Jesus said, "behold, I am with you always, to the end of the age" (Mt. 28:20).

Jesus' final encouragement to a group of people whose world had been turned upside down and inside out was to trust Him, to focus on Him, and not on their circumstances. They had been on an emotional roller coaster; they believed Jesus to be the Messiah who would save the world, only to then see Him arrested and crucified. Their pain and confusion must have been nearly unbearable. Then three days later He was alive; then they saw Jesus ascend into heaven, reminding them that He is with them always.

Jesus had left them before when He died on the cross, at least it must have seemed that way when He was crucified. Yet now He promised that He will never leave them, even though He was ascending out of their sight and is clearly no longer physically present. How can that be? Through the presence of the Holy Spirit, Jesus is constantly and fully present with us. Not just *with* us, but *in* us. Jesus has made His home *in* the people of God. He goes where we go. We only need to realize it, to ask, to pray, to be open to the possibility—the reality that He actually is who He says He is. Who is He? James said that God is a farmer.

> *"Be patient, therefore, brothers, until the coming of the Lord. See how the farmer waits for the precious fruit of the earth, being patient about it, until it receives the early and the late rains" (James 5:7).*

God is a farmer who is raising a crop of spiritual fruits in our lives. Is God just farming you and me? Is He farming St. Paul's? Is He only farming Christians? Or is He farming humanity? He planted Jesus in this world, and His Christ crop is growing. There are good seasons and bad seasons. God's crop of spiritual fruits is destined to dominate the world. And that's a good thing because God is good! Christ's mission is to change the character of humanity, to reflect and reproduce the character of Jesus in humanity, in us. His goal is to reach the whole world, every nation, every person.

He is still working on it. No one is unreachable. God's specialty is changing hearts and minds. God changed the hearts and minds of the biblical heroes. All were ordinary people, lost people, unhappy people. God specializes in turning enemies into friends. So, said James, *be patient. Establish your hearts*. An established heart is rooted and grounded in the things of God. It takes time with God in the Word, in prayer, and in fellowship, to receive, grow, and master inner strength from the Holy Spirit. God tells us that neither time nor circumstances can take God away from us. God will prevail.

James said, "Do not grumble against one another." Don't complain about each other. Why not? There's plenty of justifiable reasons to lodge complaints. To complain is to accuse, and Satan is described in the Bible as the accuser. Accusation is the way that Satan works. When we accuse one another we are doing Satan's work. Satan's disciples are masters of complaint and accusation.

Rather than complain about the world, we should praise God. Find reasons to praise God in every situation. Be thankful, even under duress. As an example, said James, take the prophets. Did the prophets complain? Yes they did. But notice that they complained to God, not to one another. They complained in prayer. And their complaints were substantial. The world was a mess, and is still a mess! What should we do about it? Pray to God about it. Pray hard. Pray regularly. Pray faithfully. Pray passionately.

Notice also that the prophets always found hope in spite of their circumstances, and that their hope stirred them to joy. Their hope was beyond their circumstances, but not beyond God's reach. In the midst of horrendous circumstances the prophets found hope and joy. Hope and joy are gospel fuel. They are gas in the gospel tank, power for the gospel grid. Hope and joy move the gospel forward. Thanks be to God!

Heavenly Father, we are so grateful for the blessings of your love and grace and mercy and wisdom, and for your presence in our lives and in the church. We give you thanks that we are able to gather and lift up the name of Jesus Christ in worship. Fill us with your joy. Connect us with your spirit. Help us to be the people that you've called us to be, because when we can do that we will be truly fulfilled.

We give you thanks Father for the taste of those things that you have given us personally and as a church. And we pray for this world, this sin soaked and broken world. We pray for the cessation of war. We pray that the drums of war would cease and would be turned into drums of celebration for your presence in our lives.

We pray for those who don't know you and we pray for the pouring out of your Holy Spirit to reach and touch people everywhere. Your specialty, Father, is changing hearts and minds and we all know that our hearts and minds need to be changed, even the best of us. So we pray for that continuing mission.

And we pray for you to bless your church and the whole world Father. For those who are faithful, give them give them power, give them the ability to communicate your Word and your love righteously and passionately and completely. And we pray that you would continue your mission in this world, that your church would continue to grow and that you would have a great harvest of the fruits of the Spirit, Father. We pray for families as they get together and contemplate getting together and make contact with one another over the holidays. And we pray for families because families are in need of healing and renewal. Every family is broken in one way or another. As we get together there are tensions and difficulties that stir us in spite of the fact that we are also filled with love and happiness to see our people. For many people Christmas is blue. It's a hard time, loved ones have been lost, children have been lost, parents have been lost, friends have been lost. And this season brings to us all of those memories. So heal us, Father, and help us to find the joy of the Lord that is beyond our circumstances.

We pray that you would heal this nation. Heal the divisions that we have in our families and our churches, in our politics, and our businesses. And we pray that you would open ears and eyes and hearts and minds for people to see the truth of your Word, the goodness of your Word. All of this, in your name. Amen.

The Mirth Of Christ: Hearkening

10 Again the Lord spoke to Ahaz: 11 "Ask a sign of the Lord your God; let it be deep as Sheol or high as heaven." 12 But Ahaz said, "I will not ask, and I will not put the Lord to the test." 13 And he said, "Hear then, O house of David! Is it too little for you to weary men, that you weary my God also? 14 Therefore the Lord himself will give you a sign. Behold, the virgin shall conceive and bear a son, and shall call his name Immanuel. 15 He shall eat curds and honey when he knows how to refuse the evil and choose the good. 16 For before the boy knows how to refuse the evil and choose the good, the land whose two kings you dread will be deserted. —*Isaiah 7:10-16*

18 Now the birth of Jesus Christ took place in this way. When his mother Mary had been betrothed to Joseph, before they came together she was found to be with child from the Holy Spirit. 19 And her husband Joseph, being a just man and unwilling to put her to shame, resolved to divorce her quietly. 20 But as he considered these things, behold, an angel of the Lord appeared to him in a dream, saying, "Joseph, son of David, do not fear to take Mary as your wife, for that which is conceived in her is from the Holy Spirit. 21 She will bear a son, and you shall call his name Jesus, for he will save his people from their sins." 22 All this took place to fulfill what the Lord had spoken by the prophet: 23 "Behold, the virgin shall conceive and bear a son, and they shall call his name Immanuel" (which means, God with us). 24 When Joseph woke from sleep, he did as the angel of the Lord commanded him: he took his wife, 25 but knew her not until she had given birth to a son. And he called his name Jesus.

—*Matthew 1:18-25*

Ahaz became king at the age of 20 and ruled from 731 to 715 B.C. Ahaz was an evil king that did not walk in the path of his godly father King Jotham (2 Chronicles 27:2). And because of his rebellion against God, the nation came to ruin about 721 B.C. with the destruction of the Temple (Isaiah 7–10). Ahaz loved the glamour and prestige of the Assyrians. In 732 B.C. he went to Damascus to swear homage to Tiglath-Pileser and his gods. When he returned he built an altar in Jerusalem like one he saw in Damascus, and also made changes in the arrangements and furniture of the Temple, "because of the king of Assyria" (2 Kings 16:18).

He burned incense in the Valley of the Son of Hinnom, and sacrificed his children in the fire, according to the abominations of the nations whom the Lord had cast out before the children of Israel. Human sacrifice was one of the most terrible sins of Palestine, and because of Ahaz it became an all-to-common aspect of religious worship in Jerusalem (Jer. 7:31; 19:2–6; 32:35; Ezekiel. 16:20, 21). King Ahaz also encouraged polytheism (2 Chronicles 28:3-4; 2 Kings 16:3). In short, he was a bad king.

Isaiah was writing to this king on behalf of God. Isaiah said that God told Ahaz to ask for a sign, so that Ahaz would know for sure that God was talking to him. Ahaz refused, citing Scripture as his reason. Let that sink in: Ahaz refused to do what God asked. He would not listen to God.

This is the context of Isaiah's message regarding this ancient prophecy of the coming of Messiah. God gave the prediction of the Messiah to a faithless king who would not listen, who is in Matthew's lineage of Jesus (Matthew 1:1-17). Isaiah then said,

> *"Hear then, O house of David! Is it too little for you to weary men, that you weary my God also?" (v. 13).*

Isaiah essentially said, *Whether you want it or not, whether you hear it or not, the Lord himself will give you a sign!* And here is that sign:

> *"Behold, the virgin shall conceive and bear a son, and shall call his name Immanuel" (v. 14).*

Immanuel means *God with us*, God in human flesh, born an infant from a virgin. The virgin represents purity, and the child, whose Father was not human, not in our human lineage, would not be subject to the curse of humanity that had been given in the garden of Eden. That's the purpose of Jesus' divine Father. It puts Jesus outside of that lineage which inherited original sin. It all points to the dual nature of Jesus who is both human and divine.

> *"He shall eat curds and honey when he knows how to refuse the evil and choose the good" (v. 16).*

That is an odd verse and it is an odd place for the Lectionary to stop the reading. The message is that Jesus will eat curds and honey and know right from wrong. He was born as a baby, but as He matures, He will eat solid food, curds and honey, as He is weened from milk. As He grows more mature, He will be able to tell the difference between right and wrong, between good and evil. The prophecy paints a Romantic picture of Jesus, suitable for Christmas.

But that's not actually what Isaiah was saying. Isaiah was predicting judgment on Israel. Isaiah was saying that the kingdom of Ahaz was about to be destroyed.

> *"In that day every place where there used to be a thousand vines, worth a thousand shekels of silver, will become briers and thorns" (v. 23).*

The Temple was destroyed in 721 B.C. when Ahaz was on the throne. And for the Jews in Jesus' time the prediction of the coming of Messiah similarly included God's judgment on the Temple that Messiah would bring. And sure enough, about forty years after Jesus's death, Jerusalem and the Temple were destroyed by Rome in A.D. 70. The Temple had been destroyed several times before, but following Jesus it would never be rebuilt. Jesus brought the final destruction of the Temple.

But not the destruction of faithfulness to God. We know now that Jesus Christ is God's eternal Temple (John 2:21). The destruction of the Jewish Temple was at the same general historic period of time the birth of Christianity.

"Uzziah the father of Jotham, Jotham the father of ***Ahaz****, Ahaz the father of Hezekiah" (Matthew 1:9).*

Consider these odd facts: Ahaz, the bad king, is in the lineage of Jesus! Matthew tells us about the birth of Jesus, predicted by Isaiah. Mary was a virgin, yet pregnant. Matthew was saying that Immanuel (Jesus Christ) would be born to a faithless generation just like during Ahaz's reign. The biblical message was that God was coming to a faithless generation in a faithless world, in spite of the fact that people were *not* listening to God.

Where God goes His judgment also goes, which means that the coming Messiah would bring God's judgment. Judgment is not necessarily a bad thing. To judge is to evaluate, and God's evaluation is righteous, right, always correct and true. God's people honor God's judgment, God's evaluation, God's values and priorities. This is what faithfulness is, nothing more, nothing less.

Faithful Christians are to think God's thoughts, see with God's eyes, hear with God's ears, and speak with God's mouth. This is what Jesus did. This is the character of Jesus Christ. And this is what Christians are to emulate, to copy, to imitate. And this emulation of Jesus is the eternal message and hope of Christmas. This emulation is the expression, the coming, of God's love in the world.

We are to imitate Jesus, imitate Paul, imitate the apostles. And this emulation or imitation of Jesus is the eternal hope of the message of Christmas because this expression is the coming of God's love in the world. It came back then. It's coming now. It will come again. It is not something that only prophets or mystics do. It not something that only pastors, deacons, and elders do. It is what all Christians are to do. All Christians are to think God's thoughts. How? By reading the Bible. All Christians are to see with God's eyes, hear with God's ears, and speak with God's mouth. All Christians are to know and abide by the Bible.

At Christmas we celebrate the birth of Christ. What does this mean today?

"Now you are Christ's body, and individually members of it" (1 Corinthians 12:27).

"For just as we have many members in one body and all the members do not have the same function, so we, who are many, are one body in Christ, and individually members one of another" (Romans 12:4-5)

"For even as the body is one and yet has many members, and all the members of the body, though they are many, are one body, so also is Christ" (1 Corinthians 12:12).

"There is one body and one Spirit, just as also you were called in one hope of your calling" (Ephesians 4:4).

The celebration of the birth of Christ is the celebration of the life of Christ in the world, not just the life of Jesus the man, but the life of Jesus Christ, who is eternal, and since His birth He is eternally present in this world.

"For God, who said, 'Let light shine out of darkness,' has shone in our hearts to give the light of the knowledge of the glory of God in the face of Jesus Christ. But we have this treasure in jars of clay, to show that the surpassing power belongs to God and not to us" (2 Corinthians 4:6-7).

We are jars of clay to be filled with the Spirit of Jesus Christ.

"For through the law I died to the law, so that I might live to God. I have been crucified with Christ. It is no longer I who live, but Christ who lives in me. And the life I now live in the flesh I live by faith in the Son of God, who loved me and gave himself for me" (Galatians 2:19-20).

"according to the riches of his glory he may grant you to be strengthened with power through his Spirit in your inner being, so that Christ may dwell in your hearts through faith—that you, being rooted and grounded in love" (Ephesians 3:15-17).

"To them God chose to make known how great among the Gentiles are the riches of the glory of this mystery, which is Christ in you, the hope of glory" (Colossians 1:27).

God has made a way in Christ, not to escape God's judgment (no one escapes God's judgment), but to fulfill God's promise. God has made a way for God's people to live *in* God's judgment, to live *by* God's judgment, to live *according* to God's evaluation of right and wrong, good and evil. Christians are called to embrace Jesus Christ, to imitate Christ in their own lives, not perfectly (who could?), not completely (not yet), but genuinely, faithfully, and adequately. How? Through the power and presence of the Holy Spirit through regeneration.

We are to live by God's judgment, to live according to the judgment of God, according to the evaluation of God, according to God's understanding of what is right and what is wrong, what is good and what is evil. And as Christians we are called to embrace, to live the life of Christ in our own life. We can't do it under our own power, so the only way that we really can do it is through the power of the presence of the Holy Spirit through regeneration. God sent Jesus Christ, who sent the Holy Spirit to us, to the church, to inhabit His people. God's Spirit, the Holy Spirit, inhabits God's people. To in-habit is to make a habit of, to habitualize behavior.

Old habits are hard to shake. Good habits are even harder to develop. But it is through repetition, discipline, and practice that it is possible to form and to maintain new habits. Old bad habits can be changed. Old bad habits are detrimental to our health, detrimental to our well-being. But those kinds of habits can be broken. They can be changed with enough determination and a smart approach.

But here's the thing: You can't change something with nothing. You can't substitute nothing for a bad habit. If you just think, *well I'm just going to stop doing that.* It isn't going to work because there is no substitution there. You have to substitute a good habit for a bad habit. You have to have something active to engage in as you are doing that. To achieve a goal we need goals that are specific, measurable, action oriented, realistic, and time bound. How do people do this? We must:

- Set a goal: be specific. Name and aim at manifesting the character qualities of Jesus Christ, the fruits of the Spirit (Galatians 5:22-23).
- Associate a habit with your goal. Be patient, don't get angry or frustrated. Think before you speak.

- Be motivated. Set up a system of rewards and punishments.
- Start small, but be consistent.
- Think long term. It takes time.
- Expect difficulties. Don't give up.

Start by changing some specific behavior. Do something different. Tell people about what you are doing; find an accountability partner. Report your progress in a journal. Talk honestly to God through prayer, thinking about God, reading the Bible. Worship regularly, and find a way to help others.

We begin by hearkening, by listening attentively for God and to God. To hearken is to give heed; to listen; to lend the ear; to attend to what is uttered in order to obey or comply. May we all grow in our ability to be like Jesus. Can you hear me now?

Precious Lord, we are so grateful for the blessing that you have provided, for your love and mercy and wisdom. We ask that you continue to provide and supply these things. Strengthen us, Heavenly Father. Help us to be who you have called us to be, as individuals, as families, as a church, as a nation, as your people.

Again, Lord, we are grateful for our church fellowship and we pray that you would help us to be faithful. Help us to understand that the best evangelism technique that we have is our simple faithfulness. May that light shine in the darkness of the world.

Lord, continue to guide us. We know that you are good, and that the things that you want for us are good, even in the midst of the things that we see in the world that are dark and awful—and there are a lot of them! So help us to be thankful that we recognize that those things in the world that are evil and awful because our recognition of that is a sign of your Holy Spirit with us.

We pray for people that don't recognize that these things are evil and awful. We pray that you would send your Holy Spirit to awaken hearts and minds, give people your judgment, your evaluation. Help us, especially your pastors all over the nation, all over the world. Help them all to preach your truth, to live your truth, to be good examples, and to provide for people what they need to respond to the things in this sinful world with faithfulness.

Open the ears of many people during this Christmas and New Year season, a time when the world lifts up Christ, lifts up Christmas. Yes, too many people do it in too many bad ways, we understand that. But you are in it, Lord, you are in our Christmas confusion. And so we pray for the light of your love, the light of your grace, your glory, your presence to shine through all of the Christmas kitsch, through all of the junk that goes on in the name of Christmas, shine through it, Father. Touch hearts and minds with the truth of Jesus Christ.

And help us to be grateful in the midst of all things, especially as we get together with family and friends, or not. For many it will be a time of sore memories, of families and friends who have been lost, husbands and wives, and brothers and sisters, and aunts and uncles, and all of that. It's part and parcel of the Christmas season because we are flooded with all of these memories, Father.

So give us the strength to see it through. And help us to be the hands and feet, the eyes and ears, the mouthpiece of Christ, as best we are able in the midst of our family situations.

The Christmas season is often filled with tension and difficulty, with people that we haven't seen for a while, people that we have history with, people who trouble us and whom we trouble. But we pray that you would grease the skids, that you would pave the way, that you would provide for us, and provide for them, and provide for reconciliation for us all. For that truly is the message of Christmas. In Jesus' name, amen.

December 18, 2023

The Mirth Of Christ: Human

*Long ago, at many times and in many ways, God spoke to our fa-
thers by the prophets, 2 but in these last days he has spoken to us by
his Son, whom he appointed the heir of all things, through whom
also he created the world. 3 He is the radiance of the glory of God
and the exact imprint of his nature, and he upholds the universe by
the word of his power. After making purification for sins, he sat down
at the right hand of the Majesty on high, 4 having become as much
superior to angels as the name he has inherited is more excellent than
theirs. … 2:5 For it was not to angels that God subjected the world
to come, of which we are speaking. 6 It has been testified somewhere,
"What is man, that you are mindful of him, or the son of man, that
you care for him? 7 You made him for a little while lower than the
angels; you have crowned him with glory and honor, 8 putting everything in subjection under his feet." Now in putting everything in subjection to him, he left nothing outside his control. At present, we do
not yet see everything in subjection to him. 9 But we see him who for
a little while was made lower than the angels, namely Jesus, crowned
with glory and honor because of the suffering of death, so that by the
grace of God he might taste death for everyone. 10 For it was fitting
that he, for whom and by whom all things exist, in bringing many
sons to glory, should make the founder of their salvation perfect
through suffering. 11 For he who sanctifies and those who are sancti-
fied all have one source. That is why he is not ashamed to call them
brothers, 12 saying, "I will tell of your name to my brothers; in the
midst of the congregation I will sing your praise."*

—Hebrews 1:1-4; 2:5-12

Jesus was born in Bethlehem, and Bethlehem was the hometown of King David, Israel's greatest king. And oddly enough, Bethlehem never really became much of anything. It was never an influential city, and yet God chose this little town, out in the country, out in the middle of nowhere, as the birthplace for the Messiah, who would be the ruler of Israel.

Micah 5 was quoted by the chief priests and teachers of the law when Herod asked about the birth of the Messiah (Matthew 2:5-6).

> *"But you, Bethlehem Ephrathah, though you are small among the clans of Judah, out of you will come for me one who will be ruler over Israel, whose origins are from of old, from ancient times." 3 Therefore Israel will be abandoned until the time when she who is in labor bears a son, and the rest of his brothers return to join the Israelites. 4 He will stand and shepherd his flock in the strength of the Lord, in the majesty of the name of the Lord his God. And they will live securely, for then his greatness will reach to the ends of the earth. 5 And he will be our peace..." (Micah 5:2-6).*

It was foretold in the ancient scriptures that Jesus would be born in Bethlehem, which literally means *the house of bread*. And so from eternity past, Jesus came into the house of bread to provide the bread of life (John 6:35). Micah's prophetic voice declared that though Jesus came from Bethlehem, He did not begin there. He began in eternity past. John says it this way:

> *"In the beginning was the Word, and the Word was with God, and the Word was God. 2 He was in the beginning with God. 3 All things were made through him, and without him was not any thing made that was made. 4 In him was life, and the life was the light of men. 5 The light shines in the darkness, and the darkness has not overcome it" (John 1:1).*

2022 years later, the darkness has still not overcome it. Knowing that Jesus comes from everlasting, not just from Bethlehem, but from everlasting, points us to several things.

First, it shows us the glory of Jesus Christ, because Jesus Christ is far more than just a man. It shows us the love of Jesus that He would leave the glory of heaven, leave His divine being, if you will, to come down to earth and wallow with us in the mud, living lives like we live. It also shows us the sympathy of Jesus, that He remained fully man and fully God at the same time, and it also shows us the nature of Jesus, that He would add humanity, the humility of humanity to His deity.

Now, of course, early on in this story of Jesus' birth, we find Matthew's lineage of Jesus, showing that Jesus has come from all of these various people. Matthew's lineage is very interesting in a number of ways. God is communicating something very important to us in the way that He arranged this chronology. First of all, typically, Jewish genealogies did not include or mention women. You can go back to the Old Testament lineage lists, and they just don't include the women. They only listed men as the head of the households, and of course, women in the Old Testament world had little agency and very little voice in spiritual matters as well.

Matthew on behalf of God, in telling the story through women like Mary and Elisabeth and Anna, is telling us that His Kingdom is a different kind of kingdom. And even in this small and seemingly insignificant detail of listing four women in Jesus' family tree, Matthew is communicating something powerful.

We are going to explore a few of those women. Consider Tamar, an Old Testament woman, daughter of Judah, and the wife of Er, who was one of the two sons of Judah. And the way that Judah's sons were born is interesting. It helps us to understand something important because these sons were the result of a adulterous relationship that Judah had with a Canaanite woman. Er was not a good husband, and he was killed by God. When he died, as was the custom at the time, the next oldest brother would marry the widow in order to continue that family lineage. The next oldest brother was Onan, who was to marry Tamar in order to continue the family lineage. But in a greedy attempt to set himself up for a richer inheritance, Onan refused to conceive a baby with Tamar, and as a result, God struck Onan dead (Genesis 38-39).

The next brother was a lot younger, which caused Tamar to wait a long time for Judah to give his youngest son to be her husband. In fact, this never happened. Judah was reluctant because he believed that Tamar was somehow cursed by God. So Tamar then took things into her own hands. She disguised herself as a prostitute and placed herself in a major roadway where she would encounter Judah, her father-in-law.

One day, Judah saw her and propositioned her. They engaged, and as a result of this liaison they conceived more than once, actually. So this was an on-going thing. In an interesting twist, then, Judah discovered that she was pregnant, and wanted to put her to death to cover up his sin, and for violating her oath to stay chaste until she remarried. But she proved to him that it was his children that she bore. She caught Judah by surprise and implicated him in this sin soaked intrigue. But in spite of all of this, one of her two sons, Perez, would be listed as an ancestor of David, and eventually in the lineage of Jesus by Matthew. This is really mind-boggling when you dig into it.

So Judah and Tamar's place in the family lineage of Jesus shows us an interesting juxtaposition between the powerful and the powerless. The hypocritical king Judah had lied about his sin. He then exploited his daughter-in-law to satisfy his own passions, and then sought to murder Tamar to hide his guilt. This is the lineage of Jesus. In Jesus' new family, both the religious hypocrite and the exploited mistress find their place in God's grace.

Rehab is also in the line of Jesus' genealogy. And the story of Rehab is equally sordid. This story took place when Joshua was conquering the promised land. When the Jewish spies came to scout out the land of Jericho, to gather information prior to Joshua's attack, Rehab was the one who hid them and protected them. She gave them shelter so that they could do their spying and get back to Joshua with their information.

She apparently had heard of the miracles of God that He had done for Israel when they were in the wilderness. And she found herself attracted to that God. She could tell that God was powerful. But she was a prostitute, a professional woman, if you will. She was exploited for her body; she sold her body for profit.

Joshua's spies stayed in her home, used her home as a base for their spying. And when the government police came to inquire about the Jewish spies, she lied to them and gave the spies cover so that they could escape. Because she helped to provide critical intelligence that helped Israel to defeat Jericho, Rehab was then given safe harbor during Joshua's attack on Jericho, and was grafted into the Jewish nation.

James, the brother of Jesus, said that her actions were evidence of her newfound faith. Her life was evidence that God is always bringing in outsiders, those seen by the religious institutions to be so damaged by exploitation and sin that they would be socially outcasts.

There are more interesting and odd stories burred in Jesus' genealogy, but that's enough for now. We may handle these other stories at some other Christmases. What we learn from all this is that the story of Jesus' lineage is not so much his coming out of a strict Jewish heritage, but that He is utterly human. Jesus comes out of humanity with all of the sins and ugliness of humanity. Jesus arises out of that. That is His humanity. The theologians say that Jesus was fully human, and being fully human means being part of the sordid history of humanity.

Angels appeared to the shepherds the night that Jesus was born. This is interesting, too, because shepherds were at the lowest end of the society. They were down at the bottom rung of society. Nobody wanted to be a shepherd. They were the poorest of the poor.

In Jewish tradition (the *Mishnah*), a belief had arisen that the Messiah would be revealed from the Migdal Eder ("the tower of the flock"). The tower had been built so that the shepherds could oversee a large flock. This gave them an elevated view of the fields, which helped them handle a large flock. The sheep of that large flock belonged to the temple, and the sheep that pastured there were temple-flocks. They were sheep meant for temple sacrifice.

God had a purpose for this shepherd audience. Their elevated view gave them access to see the fields around the stable in which Jesus was born. And the work they performed suggests the reason that God used them in the story of Jesus' birth. These men who watched the sheep that were meant for Temple slaughter received a divine message about the ultimate Lamb who would take away the sins of the world through His sacrificial death and resurrection. By using those particular shepherds God aimed the announcement of Jesus' birth directly at the Temple.

Jesus was born in a stable. Why was this? God wanted to show us that Jesus came to bring salvation to everyone, not just the rich and powerful, but also the poor and downtrodden. God's love extends to the whole human race! And Jesus showed us the depth of God's love by willingly leaving heaven's glory and sharing in our poverty. The Bible says,

> *"For you know the grace of our Lord Jesus Christ, that though he was rich, yet for your sakes he became poor, so that you through his poverty might become rich" (2 Corinthians 8:9).*

Because Jesus was born into a poor family, we can be assured that Jesus understands what it means to be poor . He came as an ordinary man to an ordinary family.

The other interesting and significant thing of this whole story is about Mary's faithfulness. Mary, the mother of Jesus, lived at a time when over two decades of war between the Roman empire and Israel had pretty much destroyed people's lives. People's farmlands and homes were desolate. Israel was a conquered and occupied territory. The economy was terrible. And crime was at an all time high. Politics could not get anymore corrupt, and there was no such thing as protection from the government. Does any of this sound familiar? This is the world into which Mary carried Jesus.

Caesar Augustus, having won a recent war, became emperor of Rome and brought stability and economic wealth—as well as impossibly high taxation in order to pay his war bills. This is why Luke tells us that Caesar Augustus mandated a census so that tax could be collected.

Mary was from the tribe of Judah and the lineage of David. This was a fulfillment of Old Testament prophecy. Mary was poor and lived in a small town. Mary was uneducated according to the standard of our world, but she knew God personally for herself, on her own. We see this in her prayer life as she dealt with her pregnancy. Mary was in the first stage of marriage.

In Jewish practices, marriages had three stages. The first step was the signing of the contract. The couple was betrothed; they were considered to be married because their engagement sealed their promises, but were not permitted to have sex. That's why the Bible says she was betrothed. A legal betrothal could only be broken by death or divorce. And this is why although they had not yet engaged in sex, Joseph was going to divorce her. But then an angel visited him and he changed his mind.

How old was Mary when she gave birth to Jesus? Betrothal usually happened right after puberty so Mary was likely in her early-to-mid teens when she became pregnant and gave birth to Jesus. Due to her pregnancy Mary did not enter the second stage of marriage until she was pregnant with Jesus. In this stage, the marriage was consummated. And in the final stage, a celebratory feast was held. Mary and Joseph had other children, so Jesus also had half-siblings.

Jesus was Mary's first born. She had four sons and an undisclosed number of daughters (Mark 6:3; Matt 13:55, 56). The Old Testament tradition was that the first born of every kind was to be dedicated to the Lord. God could trust Mary, trust that she would care for this young baby Jesus who would be no ordinary child. He was ordinary in His humanity, but extraordinary in human history.

Mary had strong faith in order to face the prospect of being an unwed mother. Mary was a prayerful person. Mary did not object to the message of the angel, but replied,

> *"Behold, I am the handmaiden of the Lord; let it be done to me according to what you have said" (Luke 1:38).*

Be like Mary.

December 25, 2022

Made in the USA
Middletown, DE
26 April 2024

53523217R00116